GHOST STALKER

A
An

GHOST STALKER

A psychic medium visits
America's most haunted sites

Michelle Whitedove

WHITEDOVE PRESS

In some instances the names have been changed to protect individuals privacy

WHITEDOVE PRESS
PO Box 550966
Fort Lauderdale FL 33355

www.MichelleWhitedove .com

To order additional Copies of this book 1-800-444-2524

Book Design by ColorCraft 954-345-1002

Photography by Maliena Slaymaker

Printed on Acid Free/Recycled paper
Printed in the USA

Library of Congress Control Number: 2002112743

ISBN# 0-9714908-3-X

First Edition

10 9 8 7 6 5 4 3 2 1

I dedicate this book

To the Great Spirit and my unseen support team,
My humble appreciation for your constant protection and
guidance during this trip, and for entrusting me with the gift of
communicating with souls who are wayward and the spirits in
the next realm called Heaven.

To the Ghosts that we encountered,
My grateful thanks for sharing your stories and allowing us to a
look at life that exists between heaven and earth. I pray that you
will find your way to the light so that your souls may be at peace.

Special thanks:

To Maliena Slaymaker,
Who was instrumental in research, location inquiries,
photography, and most importantly for her bravery and the
efficient recording of the events as they happened on this
haunted journey. I know this book would not have been
complete without your assistance and I cannot express enough
gratitude for your help and devotion to this project.

To Shanté,
Who accompanied me on this adventure, your faith in my
abilities never ceases to amaze me. I am grateful for such a
dear friend, a vessel of love, that I believe God placed in my
life to help me fulfill my mission. You know and understand me
like no one else.

To Aileen Apple,
For the vast amount of time she devoted to editing, I thank you
for your valuable contribution and perfectionism.

CONTENTS

The Stalker

Night foretells of ancient evil,
Coursing through the fear of people,
Ghosts that roam through dim lit halls,
Can you hear their hollowed calls?
Ghost Stalker, Ghost Stalker do you have the key
Ghost Stalker, Ghost Stalker who dares hunt for me

Graveyards filled with so much sorrow,
A place of death with no tomorrow,
"Lady Lost", sings a mournful song,
Of wicked men and babes long gone.
Ghost Stalker, Ghost Stalker I'm a dead solider of war
Ghost Stalker, Ghost Stalker who knocks on my door

The sky is violet and haze fills the air,
These ghosts will start wandering so seekers beware,
Specters are haunting cursed lands to this day,
Distressing the living who find them astray.
Ghost Stalker, Ghost Stalker can you save this poor soul?
Ghost Stalker, Ghost Stalker my death is now told.

- Maliena Slaymaker

BETWEEN WORLDS

*G*host stories have been around for as long as most of us can remember: scary tales told around a campfire's glowing embers, accompanied by the distant chirping of crickets. Little girls at late-night slumber parties, fantasizing about yellow ribbons wrapped around young ghostly throats; terrifying legends associated with specific locations; tales of demonic possessions-everyone knows someone who has been traumatized by such an event. So, how did these ideas about supernatural beings arise, and why do they continue to survive? All legends are based on some sort of truth, even if it is far-fetched, and from that truth, we create images in our minds of the unknown, which are usually far worse than the reality...Usually!

Many young children fear "the bogeyman" who could possibly be hiding inside their closets, or crouching beneath their beds. The frightening Hollywood versions of ghosts, evil entities, zombies, and blood-sucking vampires, have caused youngsters all over the country to ask, "Could they be real?" The movie, *Poltergeist*, undoubtedly caused the premature demise of a large number of toy clowns. To this day, my best friend can tell you, in remarkably vivid detail, about the ghost of a long-dead prom queen, still haunting the woods behind her cousin's childhood home. And how many of us have had the feeling of being watched by something unseen?

As we grow up, these thoughts begin to fade into logical absurdities; we decide that these stories of ghosts and goblins were nothing more than exaggerated tales, meant to shock the young and naïve. While some adults might retain these early memories as tucked-away nightmares, others seek to conquer their childhood terrors, by trying to understand more about ghosts and other unearthly creatures, reportedly existing among us. It doesn't matter if you are a believer, seeker, or scoffer, very few of us have gone through life untouched by the supernatural: a cold chill from an unseen source; a pet who appears to be watching an invisible creature travel around the room; a familiar smell coming from a mysterious origin; a whisper in the wind, heard a little too clearly. I can't tell you how many times I have jerked my head around, certain that someone is there, only to find a seemingly empty room. Most of us are unable to explain how these events occur, and because they are so spooky, we decide that we don't really want to know.

My friend, Michelle Whitedove, is a psychic, a medium, and a channel. She has dedicated her life to conveying messages from the "other side," and to using her clairvoyant talents to counsel those in need. As a **psychic**, she has the ability to tune-in to someone's energy, and receive information about his or her past, present and future; as a **medium**, she is able to contact departed loved ones, as well as various spirits on the other side, who communicate telepathically via feelings, thoughts and pictures. I must clarify the fact that not all psychics are mediums, this is considered a rare gift. As a **channel**, Michelle is able to relay messages and teachings from the highest level of the heavens, to provide knowledge for personal growth. She channels information from the Angel realm, just as the ancient prophets did during biblical times.

Imagine a woman walking into a room and sitting down next to you to have a conversation. She provides you with intimate details about her life, gives you messages to relay to people she knows, or even asks for your help with something. You are able to see and to hear her, as clearly as you do the others in the room, but suddenly you realize that this "person" is neither visible, nor audible, to anyone but you. Why? Because the woman to whom you are speaking is dead! Everyone looks at you as if you were insane. Those who think that they know you best, simply whisper, "It's just her imagination—after all, she's only a kid." This is what Michelle Whitedove experienced throughout her childhood. She was told that she had "imaginary friends," when, in fact, they were guardian angels, deceased loved ones, and, sometimes, even ghosts.

As a young girl, Michelle thought everyone could communicate with his or her spirit friends. When she grew older, she was confused by the negative reactions that other people had to her special skills. But her guardian angels and spirit guides never let her down. They showed her the path that she was meant to follow, and she was able to find the courage and strength to embrace her gifts, learning how to use them to help humanity.

During her teenage years, Michelle survived a near-death experience, which confirmed what she already knew: each of us survives the transition called death. She spent the next several years developing her talents, and was finally ready to begin her true mission in life: to educate others about the spirit world, and to let people know that there is more to life than meets the eye. Michelle accomplishes these goals by writing books, hosting a TV talk show, working with children, offering private readings, and teaching workshops throughout the country.

It was at one of these workshops in Fort Lauderdale, where I first met Michelle. Her lecture, held at a local bookstore, was entitled, "Messages from The Other Side." After describing her unique abilities, she spoke about life in the spirit world, reassuring us, from first-hand experience, that "our loved ones continue to exist...that death is a natural adaptation made by our souls." She told amazing accounts of deceased loved ones, who had come through to her with information, which she then shared with specific clients. She explained how we "shed our bodies much like unwanted clothing, before continuing our eternal journey..."

Following the lecture, Michelle circled the room, bringing psychic messages to those in attendance. Although she didn't even know my name, Michelle brought me a message from a dear friend, who had died suddenly. Michelle relayed what she saw: my friend's first name, her physical description, and most amazingly, details of her tragic death. These details were so accurate, that I started to cry, right in the middle of a room full of strangers.

That night, for the first time, I felt comforted and reassured: my friend was in heaven, happy and safe. This knowledge effectively allowed me to move ahead with my life, less fearful and angry, and better able to let go of my overwhelming grief.

From this initial meeting, I knew, beyond the shadow of a doubt, that Michelle's connection to the other side superseded anything I had ever previously encountered. It is also important to note that when Michelle delivers psychic messages to you, she does so in an exceptionally loving and caring manner, with only the purest intentions in her heart.

When she was creating *Ghost Stalker*, Michelle upheld this same integrity. As an author, teacher and spiritual guide, she has spent so much time conversing with spirits and angels, that sometimes I think she is more comfortable talking to them than to her human friends. Typically, Michelle does not communicate with ghosts, unless she is trying to help them move to the next realm, "into the light" or, when she is performing an exorcism. However, she made an exception to write this book, hoping to educate people about paranormal activity, while explaining the history behind many ghostly legends.

Working with Michelle is always an adventure: she comes into contact with the supernatural, the way most of us come into contact with the mailman. So one day, during a conversation someone said, "Why don't you plan a trip to visit some places in the United States that have the reputation for being haunted? You could use audio and video equipment to document supernatural experiences as they occur, and create a detailed travelogue." This was a fascinating idea... exploring famous locations, where Michelle could contact as many wayward spirits as possible, allowing them to unravel any untold mysteries about their lives and probably deaths, which had previously been shrouded in mystery. Soon after this discussion, three of us decided to go, Michelle, her assistant Shanté, and myself. It also occurred to us, that during our travels, we might even acquire some ghost stories of our own!

Very few historical facts were available about the ghosts supposedly haunting our prospective locations, and much of the information turned out to be inaccurate, based on legends that had been passed down for generations. Some ghosts were known only by their first names! But, as a psychic-medium, we knew that Michelle would be able to connect to any ghosts that might be in residence, and channel any information that they decided to share. Ghosts are drawn to Michelle because of her light and her abilities, and she understands the pain that they have experienced.

Sometimes, it is easy to forget that these wandering spirits were once human, with souls that are sparks of God. At the time of their physical deaths, they would not or could not "move into the light." Why did this happen? Among the various reasons given are: confusion at the moment of death; trauma from a brutal murder; addictive attachments to physical pleasures; deep devotion to loved ones; unresolved anger or revenge; places they refuse to leave; other types of unfinished business. Whatever their reasons for remaining earthbound, these ghosts become stuck, prisoners here on earth.

During our travels, we decided to include as much documented history as possible, not only for it's validation, but also so that you, the reader, can acknowledge that whether these ghosts appear fun and mischievous, or angry and cruel, each ghost encountered has it's own personal story, not just a freaky tale with which to scare you. They once had physical lives, and there were reasons why their souls are still restless. As we journeyed to these places, it was important to remember to have respect and compassion for them, while retaining a degree of caution: wayward spirits can act and feel very much like they did when they were alive and sometimes they are not very nice!

The remarkable story of our trip across America has been told in the pages of this book. It was a great honor to have had the opportunity to accompany an authentic "ghost stalker" to some very scary places.

And now, it is your turn... so, please open your minds, and put aside your preconceptions. Michelle Whitedove, your tour guide, and my greatest mentor, will now share the visions and intimate conversations that she had with the ghosts she met during our once-in-a lifetime, never to be forgotten adventure.

Enjoy the journey!

With love and respect,
Maliena Slaymaker

P.S. For actual photos and audio recordings of our trip, go to www.MichelleWhitedove.com, where they are posted for your convenience.

The intuitive mind is a sacred gift

and the rational mind is a faithful servant.

We have created a society

that honors the servant

and has forgotten the gift.

— Albert Einstein

SPIRITS THAT ROAM THE EARTH

*H*ello, my name is Michelle Whitedove. Some of you may never have heard of me, while others might have read my previous books, or come to know me more personally, through private readings, lectures, workshops or media appearances.

Ever since I can remember, I have been able to see ghosts, as well as other unearthly spirits, and to this day, I become awestruck at the sight of them. The main difference between my everyday life and the trip I am about to describe, is that this time I was the one seeking the supernatural, instead of the other way around. There are scores of supernatural phenomenon to write about, but this book is primarily dedicated to ghosts-those souls trapped in limbo, between our world and the next.

Before you venture further into our travelogue, I would like to clarify some important terms. First, and foremost, is the definition of a "ghost", also referred to as a "wayward spirit." A **ghost** is a soul or spirit, made of pure energy, which lived and died on earth as a human being. Instead of making the transition from death, and moving on to the spirit world (heaven), its soul remained on earth. The ghost usually resembles a lighter version of the way it looked in life, from its physical appearance to its personality. I have seen ghosts in all different forms: some are shy and gentle, usually staying far away from the living; some are mean and ugly, seeking vengeance on anyone crossing their paths. There has been a lot of controversy about whether or not a ghost has the ability to hurt, or possibly even kill, a living person. Although this is extremely rare, yes, it can happen-that is, ghosts can hurt you! If you are vulnerable, and confronted by a very powerful ghost, believe me, your life could be in danger. Some psychics will tell you that this is not true, that no ghost can physically harm a living person, but I have seen this happen- it has even happened to me.

Let's put it this way: it has been proven that some ghosts are capable of throwing objects around a room. I once saw a photograph of a laundry room, which a ghost had completely destroyed: everything was piled up to the ceiling, blocking the rear wall from view. Well, if a ghost can pick up a two-hundred pound washer, and toss it ten feet away, how difficult would it be for that same ghost to push someone down a staircase, or even out of an upstairs window?

Large numbers of cases exist, documenting incredible damage to people and their homes, seemingly caused by unknown forces. This type of damage, however, is probably not the work of a ghost, but of a "**poltergeist**." Are you curious about the difference? A poltergeist is an aggressive, mischievous, malevolent ghost. Poltergeists stick around, haunting specific locations that they were attached to in life, which they refuse to leave after death. Unwilling to share their space with the living, they begin to haunt these places, where they become troublesome, and unwelcome guests. This can all be very dramatic, but the truth is, poltergeists are much less common than regular ghosts.

Certain spirits cannot be considered ghosts at all, and this can become quite confusing. No, there are definitely not any "Casper-like" qualities about these beings, which are far from friendly! In fact, these are the most treacherous enemies in the paranormal world. Many people claim that these entities don't even exist- but, I assure you, they most certainly do. I am speaking about **dark entities**: horrible creatures, of different forms and degrees; vile beings who succumb to "the dark side," turning against God to join forces with the evil that has been created from mankind's fear. Over time, these entities become darker and more evil. They feed upon, and gain strength, from the fear and negative energy emitted by many humans. Despite what anyone says, these creatures are a real threat to humanity, attacking us in various ways. Often, we don't realize these dark entities are the cause of these attacks. (You will read more about this in a later chapter.)

It is important to note the distinction between dark entities and evil entities—also known as dark angels. Evil entities are spirits who were once part of the angel kingdom. God gave them the choice to stay or to leave the heavens with the archangel Lucifer. Because of this choice, they left the light and the love of heaven, to join the forces of darkness; their movements are restricted to the earth and astral planes. Some day, these dark angels will be allowed to return to the heavens, because God does not forsake any of his children. Eventually, everything returns to the light.

PARANORMAL TERMS AND EVENTS

A "haunting" is the most frequently heard paranormal term. A **haunting** happens when one or more ghosts inhabit a space, and make themselves known to the living. Hauntings occur when entities with free will are roaming the earth, residing in places, or attaching themselves to people. Because not all ghosts are bad or discontent, all hauntings are not harmful or negative. If you believe that all spirits and ghosts are evil, this is a misconception, it is simply not true. Just as in everyday life, there are good, loving people, as well as hateful ones- hauntings are the same. Some spirits are simply mischievous or bored, some are afraid to go into the light, and others are actually helpers to the living.

For example, a young couple purchased a house in Massachusetts, with which they had fallen in love. The house had originally belonged to an elderly couple, who had died some years before. Shortly after the new owners moved in, they realized that the previous owners still lived there—as ghosts! Now, this is considered a "haunting." However, the young couple reported, during an interview, that this ghostly couple was quite considerate: they would often lock the doors, if the young couple forgot to do so, or open windows in the summertime, to let in a pleasant breeze. The two couples shared the home, content with their combined living arrangements! In fact, the elderly woman often appeared in the kitchen, to smile approvingly at these new owners of her home.

While it is easy to visualize a ghost floating around a house, or picking up a lamp and tossing it maliciously, it is more difficult to address the question, "Where do ghosts reside, when they cannot be seen on earth?" It might sound ridiculous, but the answer is simple, they are "in limbo." The term limbo refers to the astral planes-the space between earth and heaven, where there are many different dimensions. As humans, we visit these astral planes often; frequently, we travel there during the dream state. We go there to work out our fears, often remembering this as nightmares. We also go to the astral planes to communicate with other entities that reside on earth, among which are ghosts. For instance, this is where a deceased family member may come to speak to you: when awake, you think it was a dream; but, actually, you were out of body.

When I am asleep, my lighter body frequently travels to the astral realms, where I help ghosts return to the heavens. (Many spiritually advanced people, I call them "light-workers"— do this type of out-of-body work, also known as "soul retrieval.") It is often easier for me to communicate with ghosts when I leave my physical body, because then I look more like they do, and they find me less intimidating. Ghosts also find it easier to communicate there, without the physical barriers of earth. Many ghosts end up on these astral planes, instead of going to heaven.

Now, to get a bit more in depth, I would like to describe a phenomenon that is regularly mistaken for a ghost. I am referring to an energy imprint, also called a "bleed-through." An **imprint** is not an actual ghost, but a holographic image of a terrible event. This event could have been a brutal murder, or some other type of horrible tragedy. It is actual history, which has left a scar, or a mark, in time and space; this phenomenon is accompanied by an audio or visual paranormal disturbance as well. It is like a movie scene, viewed over and over again, until it plays itself out. When enough time has passed, the scene gradually fades.

The following story is an example of how an imprint can occur. A woman bought a hotel in Mexico, she moved into it, in order to complete the necessary renovations. Starting the first night, at exactly 2:00 a.m., and continuing every night thereafter, she heard a woman's scream, a loud bang, and a thud, in one of the upstairs bedrooms. The first time she heard it, she thought it was an intruder. She called the police, but they found nothing. The second night, she figured it was a fluke of her imagination. But after hearing the same sounds for an entire week, she came to the conclusion that the hotel was haunted. She tried for weeks to find the source of this paranormal disturbance, with no success. During her third week, while preparing to paint a room in one of the hotel's large, upstairs suite, she had to first complete the tedious job of peeling off the old, cracked wallpaper. As she chipped away at the wall, small flakes of a rust-colored substance began to appear.

Worried that it could be building corrosion, or some sort of poisonous chemical, she took some samples to a lab, for analysis. When the results came back, the woman was shocked to discover that the rust flakes were actually bits of dried blood! Why would that much blood still remain on the wall, and who covered it up with wallpaper, instead of first washing it off? After investigating past hotel logs, and contacting a list of locals, she discovered that, thirty years earlier, a woman had been attacked and shot in that very room. Her death had never been officially reported, and the killer had walked free. There is no actual ghost roaming this hotel, but the crime was so brutal that the residual energy in the room plays out over and over, causing the murder to be reenacted. Nothing affects it, and the imprint continues every night, in exactly the same way. Eventually, this bleed-through will fade out; but, until then, anyone staying in this hotel is going to have a disturbing 2:00 a.m. wake-up call!

That was your first, and most basic tutorial on paranormal activity, now lets move on. Almost everyone has seen the movie The Exorcist. What exactly was going on with that little girl anyway? Well if you don't already know then let me elaborate. This is a Hollywood movie based on the true story of a young girl who was possessed! A **possession** happens when a ghost or a dark entity attaches itself to a human being, to whom it is attracted. The entity will dominate, and take control of the person's body, preventing that person from using his or her own free will. The only way to deal with a possession, is to find a priest, a holy man, a shaman, or a very advanced light-worker, to perform an exorcism, to rid the possessed individual of the attached spirit. An exorcism is a ritualistic ceremony, performed to remove a malevolent ghost or dark entity from a human host. Since I began this work, I have noticed that fewer and fewer people still perform them. The Catholic Church has all but lost the ability to do so, since their priests have not adequately passed down this knowledge. Even those who do know how, often refuse, because it is such dangerous work. Why is it so dangerous? Because the evil spirit possessing the body does not want to leave it, and almost always will physically attack anyone who tries to vanquish it. If the entity is forced to leave one body, it will try to take over another. Anyone who does this work requires insurmountable courage and faith, as well as physical and spiritual strength. Also important is that your connection to God must be pure and steadfast. Before I begin an exorcism, I pray for protection, and call in my entire support team to help ensure my safety, as well as that of those involved. In one particular case, I was called to a woman's home to perform an exorcism on her six-year-old son. I witnessed the child's voice suddenly change into that of an old man's, and observed that the child's personality was not his own. He had become much stronger than a normal little boy, and was threatening to cut his mother into pieces; he had become a danger to his family, as well as to himself. After the exorcism was successfully completed, the boy could not remember what he had done. He knew only that a man had been with him for a long time, making him do bad things. The family was as grateful to have their son back, as the little boy was grateful to be rid of his unwanted hitchhiker. Knowing that this family is safe and happy now, is what makes this difficult work so rewarding for me.

One of the grossest things that I have ever had to deal with, as a psychic-medium in the paranormal field, is **ectoplasm**. The textbook definition of ectoplasm is: "A visible substance believed to emanate from the body of a spiritualistic medium during communication with the dead; an ethereal substance that appears in the presence of a spirit or ghost." In all my years of work, I have experienced this phenomenon only once: during an exorcism I was performing with a Native American medicine man, we both became congested with something horribly thick and gooey. By the time the ceremony was over, this disgusting material was in our noses, ears, mouths, and even the corners of our eyes. It was as thick as mucus, and very concentrated. Both of us felt sick, and it was difficult to breathe. After leaving the house, we had to pull over at a rest stop, so we could wash the ectoplasm off of our bodies. This is an experience I hope I never have to repeat!

Since the beginning of time, man has sought to converse with loved ones on the other side; death seems so final, for the humans left behind. Grief is a natural emotion, but there is something you need to know: our departed loved ones do not grieve for us! In fact, now and then, they look in on us, and sometimes they even try to get a message through. They are curious, and want to see how we are fairing; but they know that our earthly existence is only a brief moment in the scheme of eternity. So, for those seeking to make contact with departed loved ones, I would encourage you to find a legitimate medium. Don't try to hold a séance, or purchase a Ouija board. A **séance** is a gathering of people who are trying to conjure up and communicate with the dead. People don't realize that, during a séance, you can be susceptible to dark entities coming through. These dark entities will lie, draw you into their web of deception, and make you feel more confused and upset than you were before you began. The same is true for Ouija boards. People first started to experiment with these boards, comprised of numbers and letters, around 1892. Seekers would place their fingers on a small pointer, and ask for a specific person to come forward to communicate with them. When a spirit came through, it would use its energy to direct the pointer to letters spelling out short, often obscure, messages. But how can you be sure what you are summoning, if you are placing your trust in a wooden board with painted letters? Experienced mediums know how to protect themselves; more importantly, they know the difference between dark entities, and spirits resonating love and good will.

When you think about seeing a ghost, usually you think of it in a human form-perhaps ethereal, or transparent— with a face, a body, and some type of clothing. But the fact is, a ghost is not usually seen as a person; instead, it is often seen as a white splotch, a streak of light, or a passing shadow. One of the most common images is that of an **orb**, which is a ghost taking form as a floating, luminescent sphere. Orbs can vary, in size and color, and frequently show up in photographic images. An orb is the most common mode of travel for wayward spirits. Orbs are sometimes referred to as **globules**, which are similar to orbs, but more irregular in shape. During our trip, I saw the ghosts primarily with my psychic ability: they appeared to me visually, usually I was the only one who could see them. But on several occasions, I pointed to an area and said to my companions, "Look, right there is a ghost!" We quickly snapped a photo, but what appeared in the picture was an orb replacing the human-shaped ghost that I had seen psychically.

Even if you can't see them, there are other indicators of ghostly or other paranormal activity in your vicinity. A common way to recognize when a ghost is near, is to feel the dramatic drop in temperature that occurs-sometimes, it gets cold enough for you to see your own breath! Paranormal activity almost always causes a flux in the energy: almost anything that runs on batteries or electrical currents will start to malfunction; the hands on the clock will spin; appliances and lights will flicker on and off; and compass dials will twirl in crazy circles. Some ghosts can become more physically aggressive, but it takes an enormous amount of their energy to affect us in this way. Some of the more powerful ghosts and entities can actually accumulate enough energy to move objects, throw things, brush against you, or touch you by pulling, pushing or pinching. These more experienced ghosts are able to take form, and manifest for us to see, but a sighting is rare. It is easier for most people to capture these ghostly energies on film, or with video or audio equipment. Spirits show up as light globules, orbs, shadows, light streaks, or fog. Less often, people can capture details such as facial features, colors and items of clothing that are worn, or the reflections of translucent faces in mirrors. Perhaps the most interesting aspect about these energies that are captured on film, is that when the photographer takes the picture, he often does not see anything unusual. He took a photo of an object or a place because it interested him. When the film is developed, a paranormal image appears, which had not been previously seen.

While on this ghost trip, we frequently had this type of experience. I had an advantage over the others, because of my ability to see psychically. Also, some ghosts exhibit discretion: they will make themselves appear in front of one person, but not another. If a group of people are in the same room, and a ghost appears, usually only one or two of them will see it. Just because people want to see a ghost, doesn't mean that they will. It is more common to collect photographic evidence, than to witness a manifestation.

As I stated earlier, people make contact with ghosts through Ouija boards, séances, channels, mediums, meditation and dreams. I encourage everyone to pay close attention to their dreams, because this is a way in which everyone can connect to the other side. The dream state is a doorway to the spirit world, it is a way that spirits can contact us, especially if we do not heed them in physical form. Many people tell me that they dream of deceased loved ones; I then explain to them that the person was really there, speaking to them in these dreams. Dreamtime visitations are common. But it is not necessary for you to wait for your loved ones to contact you. Obviously, as you can tell from the title of this book, people can, and do, successfully make these contacts on their own.

And now, you are ready to begin the travelogue, and decide for yourselves whether or not you believe in ghosts! It is my hope that reading about the incredible adventures to follow, will enable everyone to share in the thrill that I had while experiencing them. So, let's get started!

From Ghoulies, Ghosties and

long leggety beasties

and things that go bump in the night

Good Lord, deliver us!

– Scottish saying

GHOSTS VS. EVIL ENTITIES

*I*t was a challenge for me to put my travelogue into a format that my readers would find interesting, as well as educational. Throughout the rest of this book, the places we visited are described in the order in which they were experienced. Each chapter begins with a "haunted history," and any historical facts that were available about the destination. This background information will be helpful, later in the chapter, when you read the actual "log," or diary. At the end of each chapter, is a synopsis of my channeled information: the information I received from the ghosts I encountered, plus any clarifications I was given from my spirit guides and angels.

Now that you have some familiarity with paranormal definitions, I thought it would be appropriate to describe a few of the specific entities I have encountered, over the years. These stories are true, and represent but a small fraction of what people call, "my most unusual life." I guess it's difficult to believe, but I really do come into contact with the spirit world on a daily basis. Paranormal activity in my home has become so commonplace, that my family finds it more of a nuisance than anything else; for other families, a ghostly intrusion can be frightening, as well as confusing. I am going to share stories with you about ghosts, as well as evil entities, so that you can better understand the different ways in which they affect our lives. The next four events stand out vividly in my mind. The first two pertain to evil entities of the most demonic nature; the last two are quite ghostly indeed!

EVIL AT MY BEDSIDE

My first encounter with an evil entity occurred about ten years ago. I had been in a deep sleep for several hours, when something shook my shoulders. I awoke immediately, feeling startled and disoriented. As I gazed into the darkness, and allowed my eyes to adjust to the dim lighting of the street lamp outside, I surveyed my surroundings. At the foot of my bed I saw an enormous, black shadow! I cannot sufficiently impress upon you what I mean by "enormous." This entity was about eight feet tall, and very broad. It wore a black, floor-length cloak with a hood, which shadowed all of its facial features; its hands were folded across its chest.

Despite the fact that it was a black shadow, there was an amazing amount of definition: I could see the ripples and seams of the cloak, and features of its massive arms and torso. This entity was blacker than onyx, hollow, and completely evil. It was more horrible than anything I had ever seen. I could feel his ominous presence bearing down on me. I couldn't scream, and my chest was so heavy that I could barely breathe. I groped for my husband's arm, unable to tear my eyes away from this dreadful being. I tried desperately to shake my then husband awake, but he did not move. I felt like the shadow in front of me was somehow preventing it. This went on for several minutes. I was so confused... What did it want? Why did my guardian angels and protectors allow it into my bedroom in the first place? And, more importantly, how was I going to get rid of it? Finally, it disappeared, and I was left alone, with a pounding heart! At last, I was able to awaken my husband. He sat up, completely unaware that anything out of the ordinary had just happened. However, he could see how upset I was. He knew that I had seen something, because I could barely catch my breath, my face was pale, and my hands were shaking. Much later, after I had calmed down, I tried to get back to sleep. I began to pray for the protection of my family and myself. I asked my angels and guides why they had allowed something so evil to come to me in this frightening way. The answer I received from spirit was that they wanted me to see what they were up against— what we are all up against! Showing me this entity was a test, so that I could witness the darkness that exists on earth and on the lower astral levels. This type of evil is what they battle to protect us from every day, and what they were asking me to battle against! "Spirit" wanted me to feel the energy and visually witness this evil. They told me that they would have never allowed this entity to hurt or even communicate with me, but that it was important for me to witness the darkness in order to fully grasp the reality of it. These entities only exist here, but not in the heavens. After this experience, I began to comprehend the evil from which our angels and guides continuously protect us. I was able to walk away with a much clearer understanding and a newfound respect for my unseen support team, and what they are able to accomplish. Most of us are unaware of the many things that our "support teams" do for us on a daily basis.

EVIL ON A MOUNTAINTOP

My second experience with an evil, demonic force, occurred during a skiing trip I went on with my husband and another couple, to Colorado. This time, I wasn't lucky enough to just "see" it! The trip had gone well, but the morning of our departure proved otherwise. We woke up early, and decided to have coffee, before starting the long drive down the mountain. I was watching the snow, as it fell peacefully onto the mountaintops, when my spirit guides suddenly came to me. They told me, most adamantly, that we were all in danger of having an automobile accident that day. They said that we should not get into the car, but, if we did, we needed to at least change drivers. My friend's husband, Robert, had rented the SUV, so naturally he had been doing the driving. However, my guides insisted that he was not to drive, and that a terrible accident would happen if he did. I immediately told my friends and my husband about the warning. Of course, no one listened. I explained to Robert that I meant no offense, but it was as though he had become a different person. Mean and stubborn, he insisted that he was a good driver— and that was that! The four of us left the dinning room to go and get the car. I lagged behind with my husband, begging him to drive. He simply scoffed at me, and took his usual place in the back seat. I knew we would be in danger, but as I stood in the snow, refusing to get in, I was outnumbered. My husband became angry with me, as did both of my friends. "Michelle, get in, or we will miss our flight." "Michelle, you're acting crazy, Robert is a good driver, stop being difficult!" After a long debate, I had to decide either to get into the car, or remain alone on the mountain, not much of a choice. Reluctantly, I slid in behind the front passenger seat, next to my husband. In less than five minutes, I started to have a panic attack. I could feel the growing threat: my heart raced, and my breath became ragged, as I glanced sideways at the hazardous, icy road. I began to pray. I imagined white light, around the car and all of us inside. I called in my guides and angels for protection. For good measure, I even prayed to the saints and Jesus. I asked God to please see us to safety. It was then that I looked up, and glanced at the steering wheel. To my absolute horror, I saw that Robert's hands, which were clutching the steering wheel, had morphed into demonic, animal-like claws! They were long and hairy, with dingy nails. The morph crept up to his mid arm, as if something were taking over his whole body. At that moment, the wheel began to turn uncontrollably, from side to side. The car fishtailed, and twice almost went over the side of the mountain. The narrow, two-lane road offered only two options: the mountainside, on the right, or a sheer drop-off, with no bottom in sight, on the left. There was nothing between the road and the edge, not even a measly guardrail. Everyone panicked. I kept thinking about what my guides had said, and how far down it was to the bottom of the mountain. No one could survive such a fall! I leaned forward, and calmly whispered into Robert's ear, "Whatever you do... don't slam on the breaks!" I looked at his face, and noticed that his eyes were vacant and glazed. What I said hadn't registered, because, "no one was home." Whatever evil entity was attacking us, had taken over his body; we were all in great peril. It felt like hours, but, only a few minutes later my warning became a reality. I kept seeing a vision of someone in the car, dying. Suddenly, the SUV lurched forward, flipped over, skidded down the road, and slid into the side of the mountain. I did not have my seatbelt on, and I landed hard against the side door, Glass, luggage, and even my husband, landed on top of me. My knees buckled from the weight, and my shoulder felt like it was on fire. I was trapped! My two friends in the front climbed out, and frantically tried to flag someone down. My husband was left to try and free me. He had to throw the luggage off of me, and even then my knees were stuck between the seat and floorboard. It seemed impossible to move. Gasoline was leaking from the gas tank, and our friends screamed for us to hurry, in case of an explosion. After what seemed like an eternity, my husband was able to pull me free. I was cut and bruised; glass was trickling down my face, and I was barely able to stand, but I whipped my head around and shouted at all three of them for not heeding my warning. Thank God we all survived, and escaped with only minor injuries, but it took awhile for my anger to subside. Much later, we discussed the accident. Robert, the friend who had been driving, said that he couldn't remember anything, except suddenly losing control and then flipping over. I asked him if he remembered my advising him not to break and, as I suspected, he did not.

Later, when I prayed and asked my angels why this had happened, they had much to say. Sternly, they told me that I should never again get into a car that they had warned me against. And they meant it! They also told me that someone was meant to die that day, but, at the last moment, my angels and guides had been able to intervene. The driver of the car was agnostic at the time, and his lack of beliefs made him the evil entity's most vulnerable target. Knowing the life mission I came here for, and the fact that an opportunity for sabotage had become available, a battle between light and dark had ensued. The dark forces purposefully waged this attack, to try and rid themselves of me, a light-worker. My guides, who normally protect me from these dark entities, could do little on this occasion but forewarn me. Luckily, with all the prayer and protection that was given, the worst-case scenario did not come to pass. I should have listened to my guides the first time. It's hard to describe what it was like to see a demonic possession. To see a person, who is usually pleasant and nice, suddenly become hollow and wretched, seems surreal; it is even more horrifying when you add the visual of a textbook demon, with sharp teeth, clawed hands, and red eyes. The forces of good and evil battle against each other constantly. Usually, the people affected have no idea what has really transpired. I think it's safe to say that I will never again ignore a warning from my protectors. We would all do well to remember this: if your gut feeling says something is bad, it probably is. Trust yourself, and your guides. Evil does exist, and it can manifest in many forms.

Thankfully, it is more common to run into ghosts, like the ones I describe in the following stories. Ghosts can be dangerous, but normally not to the same degree as evil entities.

THE HOTEL ALLEGRO

Hotel History: The Hotel Allegro was originally built in 1894, as the Bismark Hotel. It was completely rebuilt in 1926.

The "Windy City" of Chicago is famous for its many cultural attractions. It is also home to a very funky, upscale, boutique property, called the Hotel Allegro, located in the theater district. The lobby area is art deco meets Alice in Wonderland, where a giant red velvet couch invites you to sit, while a DJ spins records. This hotel lives up to its name: bright, upbeat and entertaining. Soon, we would discover that it was a little livelier than expected. Shante and I arrived in the late afternoon, and managed to get the very last room. Because of a large convention, every hotel in the city was sold out. The room that we were given was very small, but attractively furnished, with two full-sized beds. After a busy day, involving airports, taxi rides, and talking business at the expo, we were ready for room service and a good night's rest.

The first night in the hotel, I experienced one of the most physical manifestations that I have ever witnessed. My friend had fallen asleep fairly quickly, but I was not to be so lucky. It took awhile for me to get used to the hard, hotel bed, but after much tossing and turning, my eyes finally became heavy. Not long after dozing off, I was awakened by a ghost, who was roaming the hotel. He woke me up very abruptly, demanded my attention. I was very tired, and I tried as best as I could to ignore his presence, hoping he would go away. This was to no avail. He began to physically tug on my bedding. I attempted to rid myself of him several times throughout the night, but not only was he strong and hostile, he was able to harass me physically. At this point, I decided to speak with him, out-of-body. To some, this will seem bizarre: when I go to sleep, I can leave my physical body, which appears to be sleeping; then, my spirit's lighter version can move about freely, wherever it chooses to go. This is called "astral travel." I am conscious in this state, and fully aware of my surroundings. In fact, in this form, I am much like a ghost, except my body is still living so I can return to it. I went to this ghost in my lighter self, to try and understand why he was so persistent with me.

As we communicated, I learned that the man had been an atheist in life, and was a bit uneducated. He had come to work on the railroad, when it was originally being laid in Chicago. I looked at his hard exterior: he was dressed in a dirty, white, button-up shirt, with its sleeves rolled up to the elbows, and blue, pinstriped overalls. He wore big rugged boots, and his hands seemed capable of snapping me in two. His face was haggard, and he had a long, gray beard, which matched his scraggly gray hair. The ghost informed me that he had worked on the railroad from the beginning of its construction. He had been in charge of engine maintenance, and of stoking the furnace that pushed the steam engines forward. His whole life had been dedicated to the rail. Chicago is famous for its elevated railroad tracks, and it so happened that one was right next to the hotel. This is where he had died, but how this happened, he would not say. This man had been stuck in his ghostly form for a very long time, unable to move on, and unable to make contact with anyone living. He found me intriguing, because finally he had found someone who could see him! In his mind, this was his big opportunity to find help. Much confusion and helplessness surrounded his spirit, and because of his lack of faith, he could not see his angels; he was too fearful to follow the light into heaven. Instead, he roamed the hotel and the dismal astral level, clouded with the deception of his own eyes. Maybe I was the light he needed, so that he could find his way. Whether he knew this or not, he wasn't about to let me get away. When I tried to awaken from my sleep, he would immediately hound me again. His struggle to keep my attention was relentless. I woke Shante, complaining about my uninvited guest, and she growled at me in a sleepy, uncaring manner, "What does he want?" "Can't you just make him go away?"

The rugged ghost became angry. He was able to hear my conversation, and he was upset that Shante would not listen, and even more so because she had tried to rid us of him. Suddenly, my friend screamed, "Ouch, Michelle, he just pinched me." "My arm really hurts!" I turned on the lamp, and she lifted up the sleeve of her nightshirt. Sure enough, a black and blue welt had already started to form on the back of her arm. We were both shocked. (Secretly, though, I had to snicker at the reality check he had just given her!) The next day, I felt a bit more pity for her, as the bruise she received had grown larger, and darkened into an angry reminder of him.

At one point, during the chaotic night, I managed to show the ghost of the railroad man a way to move into the light. The next night was quiet, and I was able to rest comfortably, knowing his spirit was finally at peace.

THE GHOST IN RED SILK

The next story I want to share is a particularly frightening one, which took place in my own home. It was very early in the morning, about a year ago. It was 5:00 a.m., and the entire household was fast asleep. I was out-of-body, as I often am, when a strong feeling came over me, and I felt the sudden urge to return home. More specifically, I was being called to a houseguest's bedroom, but I was unsure why, or by whom. When we are out-of-body, we travel at the speed of thought. Just think of a place, and in an instant you appear there; it's common practice, and that is what I did. My lighter body walked into her room, and what I saw was ghastly. In bed, next to my houseguest, was the most evil, hideous ghost I had ever seen! He looked like a dead corpse, and he wanted to appear that way. His face was white and ashen, and his eyes were surrounded with grayish-black circles. The ghost's lips were white and pasty, his dark hair was slicked back in a greasy, sidelong part, and his red silk pajamas shone eerily. He smirked at me, and his pitch-black eyes glittered in a sadistic, menacing way that seemed to taunt me. In an instant, as his stare bore into me, I knew what this ghost meant to do. He sat up in bed with the covers pulled up to his waist. My friend, asleep on her side, was totally unaware of the vile ghost lurking beside her. He had every intention of raping her, and he had gathered enough energy so that he might have been able to do just that. I panicked! His energy hit me in the chest so hard that it hurt. He was malicious, evil, sick, and twisted. I was dazed by his sudden attack. Desperately, I tried to yell at my friend, to make her aware of the danger. In my tizzy, I had forgotten that I was in my lighter body, and that she could not hear my voice. I tried to throw different objects at her, but they simply passed through my hands. Finally, I snapped out of my hysteria and realized that I had to wake up my physical body. I sprinted from her room into my own, and jumped headfirst into my body. With a jolt, I sprang from my bed and darted through the door. I burst into my friend's bedroom, and screamed at her to wake up. She jumped up with a start, and tried to focus on what I was saying. I explained what was going on, and she became absolutely mortified! The ghost looked at me, with the same challenging stare he had when I was out-of-body. But now I was armed with the physical strength that I had lacked when I was in my lighter body. Swiftly, I cleared and blessed her room. I lit sage, and prayed, and finally his ghost was vanquished, never to return. Sometimes, I still can picture his grotesque image, and I am just so thankful that his attack was unsuccessful.

THE MARRIED GHOST

I must say, that the ghost tale closest to me has been an ongoing saga. In order to relate this story properly, it will be necessary to provide a bit of background information. By 1995, I had begun to use my psychic gifts to help others. At the time, I owned a nail salon, and it seemed that more and more frequently, when I would touch my clients' hands, I would receive personal information about them, which I would be prompted to relay. Over time, the messages became stronger and more vivid.

The first time I met Sarah, she had just moved into

town. She came to my nail shop, after finding the address in the yellow pages. When she sat down, and I took her hand in mine, I received a flood of visions. Immediately, the scene of her husband's death overcame me. It was like I had gone back in time, and was watching the events that had happened, just prior to his death. I told Sarah what I saw, and apologized profusely for my outburst. She listened intently, and then she said that she had been wishing for closure about the circumstances surrounding her husband's death, ever since it had happened, because the police had told her so little. Without hesitation, I divulged the information that I was seeing: he was on a large boat in the middle of the ocean; he was being beaten by a group of men, who finally drowned him.

Jim came to me as a ghost, and showed me what he had looked like when the Coast Guard found him, days after the drowning. The vision was so grotesque, I felt sick. His body was greenish and bloated, and decaying from the salt water that he had been floating in. A small anchor was tied to his foot, and a chunk of flesh was missing from the side of his face. Sarah was flabbergasted. The police had eventually informed her that her husband had been murdered, but they claimed to have very few leads. At one point during the investigation, Sarah had insisted that the coroner show her Jim's body. Instead, they had shown her a photograph, and the image of him was exactly as I had described. My heart went out to this woman and, almost immediately, we became good friends. I offered to accompany her to the island where her husband had been murdered, to look at the file, and offer any leads that I could. Sarah was very grateful.

Within a couple of weeks, we embarked on the first of many journeys that concerned her dead husband. When we arrived at the police station, we were told that the detective who had originally been assigned to this case was no longer at the station. A department head pulled the file for us, since it was still considered an open case. I told the officer that I felt that something else had been wrong with Jim's lungs, besides the fact that he had drowned. I also received a vision of a puncture wound. We asked if I could touch any of the evidence from the murder. They brought me his swim trunks, which had been kept in a large, plastic envelope at the police station. As I held them, I told the officer that Jim had not died in the ocean, he had been taken someplace else, and tortured for information about a drug deal, which had gone bad. I saw and described the men involved. They were dark-skinned, with dark hair and eyes. Most appeared to be Hispanic, or possibly Colombian. One man's name was Wayne. The police were shocked when they realized how accurate my information was. They confirmed that Jim's lungs had indeed been an issue, because even though he had been found in the ocean, his lungs had been filled with fresh water, not salt water! This information also validated the fact that he had been murdered on land, and then brought back to the ocean. The boat, in which Jim had gone to meet the men, had been blown up and then sunk, in a successful effort to get rid of the evidence. Unfortunately, the police were not interested in pursuing the investigation into this case. Since Jim's death, in 1991, no new leads had been found. Despite the accuracy of my information, they would not make it a priority. At the end of the day, I gave Sarah the bad news: the police would never solve Jims murder.

For Sarah, the most important aspect about this was that she received more closure from my information than she had in all the years since Jim's death. For me, this was important because I learned that Jim was a wayward spirit. He had loved life very much, and this brutal murder left his spirit in turmoil, angry that he had died. Jim began to visit his family right after he died; he refused to leave his loved ones or his material possessions.

When a person becomes a ghost, and haunts their loved ones, the ghost begins to influence them. How can a wife move on, when the ghost of her husband stays by her side, comes to her in her dreams, and wanders around her house? Over the next few months, I made several trips with Sarah to the home she had shared with Jim before he died. On our second trip, he showed us that he was aware of our efforts. We were looking around the property after dark, when suddenly thick fog from nowhere began to roll in. In an instant, Jim's ghost appeared to me out of the fog! He stood against the house, grinning at us. Sarah could see the strange fog, but she could not see Jim, although I could see him perfectly. "So," he said to me, as he looked at his wife, "look at my little Sea Cow." I became angry at this seemingly derogatory statement. I turned to Sarah and said, "Can you believe this, he just called you a Sea Cow?" Sarah's mouth fell open, and her eyes widened in shock. "Michelle" she exclaimed, "that was what Jim use to fondly call me, as a joke between us because I was always floating around in our swimming pool." "I can't believe it!" Eventually, the fog drifted away, and with it went Jim's ghost. We decided that we had had enough for one night, and headed back to our vehicle. As we drove up the road, an enormous owl flew down in front of our headlights, then swooped off into the trees. Among other things, owls represent death, so this was another confirmation of his ghost. In the following years, Jim continued to visit his family, especially through their dreams. Occasionally, I would stay at Sarah's new home, and it was not uncommon to see Jim trudging up and down the stairs, sitting next to her, or even following her out the front door. He still loved her and did not want to leave her.

Sarah made constant efforts to help her husband move into the heavens. She had a shaman perform a ceremony, and she constantly lit candles and said prayers for him. In one particular instance, Sarah decided to try and consciously travel to him in the dream state, to attempt to get him to cross over to the light. She found herself outside of a home, very similar to the one he had owned before they married. The house was empty, and she finally found him sitting on a couch in the basement, staring at a static-filled television screen. He looked at her and said, "Sarah, you rarely come to see me anymore, and my children never come to see me at all." When she woke up, she called and told me about the dream. I began to wonder about his effect on the rest of his family, who were scattered in different states. Jim's two children, from another marriage, never spoke to Sarah after his untimely death. Each family member dealt with the tragedy in their own way.

After some counseling, Sarah made a decision: she was finally going to bury Jim's ashes. Having his ashes in her house only gave his ghost that much more energy. If Sarah ever hoped to move on with her life, she would have to put him to rest, physically as well as emotionally. Shortly after Sarah sent Jim's ashes back to his hometown, to await burial, Sarah received a phone call from Jim's granddaughter, Abby. After a decade her mother, Jim's daughter-in-law, had written to Sarah to tell her about the vivid dreams that the child was having about her grandfather. And that Abby believed that her grandfather was still alive. Sarah spoke to Abby about her dreams. Abby told Sarah that after her grandfather died, even though she was only two years old, he began to appear to her in her bedroom at night. They would speak to each other, and he would play games with her. Now, at age thirteen, Abby was convinced that he was still alive.

As she grew older, Abby's dreams about her grandfather became less frequent; but in her heart she believed he was alive, and she felt that she needed to find him. Her emotions overwhelmed her; it was easy to see that the bond with her grandfather was very deep, and that their loving relationship had continued to develop, even after his death. Sarah had a long conversation with Abby, and explained to her that her grandfather was a ghost who loved his family so much that he still wanted to be a part of their lives. At first,

Abby refused to believe this. But Sarah said that if her grandfather were alive, he wouldn't be able to appear to her. This gave her something to think about. Sarah also sent Abby a copy of my first book, *"She Talks with Angels,"* which has a detailed chapter about ghosts and wayward spirits. After that, Jim's granddaughter had a better understanding of the spirit world.

A short time later, Sarah heard from Jim's daughter. She, too, was looking for closure, and she suffered from the weight of her father's death. She had dreamed that Sarah had discarded his ashes: Jim had shown his daughter some upsetting images, of his ashes being carelessly scattered away. Sarah assured her that his ashes were safe, and that she intended to bury them next to his mother, it had just taken her a long time to come to terms with her loss. I told Sarah that Jim was visiting his entire family in their dreams, and that each of them was contacting her independently, because of his prompting from the other side.

This is an excellent example about how manipulative a ghost can be. Sarah was trying to move on with her life, and had tried to convince Jim to move into the heavens. Mistakenly, Jim felt that Sarah had shunned him, and he aggressively brought his family members together, after more than a decade of no communication between them.

Jim's intention is only to be with his loved ones and continue to be involved in their lives, but his presence is both a hindrance and interference, exactly the opposite of what he is trying to achieve. Presently, Jim's spirit is still wayward. He has less of an affect on Sarah now, since she sent away his ashes and keeps her home well protected, but, from time to time, he still appears to her in her dreams with loving messages. Unfortunately, we cannot force Jim to the light. Even after all this time, he has not found peace. Sarah and I continue to pray for him, and to send him loving thoughts. When he does show himself to me, I offer him the way to the light. Some day, I hope he will decide to follow it.

Life is pleasant.

Death is peaceful.

It's the transition that's troublesome.

— Isaac Asimov

THE QUEEN MARY
LONG BEACH, CALIFORNIA

SAILING HISTORY

*T*he RMS Queen Mary was a luxury ocean liner, whose maiden voyage was on May 27, 1936. She was appropriated and refitted for wartime service, from March of 1940, until September of 1946. She returned to the seas as a luxury liner, in July of 1947.

As a passenger cruise ship, she sailed in a time when society was very aristocratic. People dressed up, from morning through evening, and they lived for parties. The Duke and Duchess of Windsor still hold the record for bringing aboard the most pieces of luggage for a single voyage; of the 155 pieces, eighty were sent to their stateroom, and the remaining seventy-five were stored in cargo.

The Queen Mary, and her sister ship, the Queen Elizabeth, helped our country win the Second World War by swiftly transporting soldiers back and forth across the ocean. Mary was the first ship to transport an entire U.S.

military division in one crossing. She still holds the world's record for the most number of people transported at one time (16,683 men). This was in July of 1943. During the war, Hitler and the Emperor of Japan offered a $250,000 bounty for the ship, plus the Iron Cross with Oak Leaves, to any submarine captains who would sink her.

The Queen Mary could reach a speed of twenty-five to twenty-nine knots (thirty-five miles per hour), but submarines could only travel at about seventeen knots, so no one could ever catch her. In 1941, the Queen Mary was nicknamed the Grey Ghost. Destroyers would escort the ship for the first 150 miles of her crossing, then when they turned back, airplanes and blimps would follow the ship, for as long as their fuel lasted. She was left to her own resources, to cross the rest of the Atlantic. The ship averaged about 15,000 men per crossing, and never took longer than five days to complete the journey. Her record, for the fastest crossing time, was three days, twenty-three hours. In February of 1946, she began her service as a "bride and baby shuttle." Throughout the war, the Queen Mary was never attacked: she never fired her guns in anger, and she never lost a single person to the enemy. During the war, she traveled more than 600,000 miles and transported more than 750,000 people.

The ship's boiler rooms were exceptionally dangerous: many men died there—from the heat, the steam explosions, and various other hazards. There were twenty-seven boiler tanks, housed in five boiler rooms, which extended along the bottom of the ship. Men used catwalks to service these tanks, which were about sixty feet tall and rose from the floor to the ceiling.

The worst accident involving the Queen Mary occurred on October 2, 1942. She was using a zigzag cruising pattern, off the coast of Ireland, and was accompanied by the HMS Curacoa, a destroyer. The Queen Mary ran into the middle of the Curacoa, and split it in half with her bow. The two halves of the Curacoa damaged both sides of the Queen Mary, as well as her front bow. The Curacoa quickly sank, and three hundred souls were lost at sea. The Queen Mary was ordered not to stop and help the sinking ship, for it was feared that if she did, she might be attacked by enemy subs, and then even more lives would be lost.

Most of the deaths, associated with the Queen Mary, occurred during the war; they were due to suicides, drowning, or common natural causes. Other deaths linked to the ship, occurred in the eras preceding and following the war.

No longer in use as a sailing ship, the Queen Mary has been turned into a "floating hotel," and has become one of Southern California's most famous attractions.

HAUNTED HISTORY

Although the entire ship is haunted, the paranormal activity is stronger in certain areas. For example, over the years, there was so much activity in Room B-340 that it was finally turned into an office, and made a part of the accounting department.

One incident was reported by a maid, who had been cleaning B-340 before it became an office. She had finished changing the bed, and walked out for a moment to get some towels. When she returned, a few minutes later, she saw that the bed linens had been tossed all over the floor! Several other maids reportedly found water running in the sinks, although no one had rented the room for days. The hotel began to check through its logs. They found that in 1966, while the ship was still sailing, a woman staying in B-340 had reported to the night steward that there was a man in her room, tugging on the bedspread. She swore that he had walked right through the solid door; but the night steward had been outside in the hall, and he had not noticed anything at all. Searching further back in the logs, they discovered that in 1948, a third-class passenger—an Englishman named Adamson had been found dead in room B-226. The cause of death was unknown. The relevance here is that B-340 had originally been B-226: the numbers had been switched, during one of the ship's numerous renovations.

Another event, reported more recently, concerns the Mayfair Room (also now part of accounting). One Saturday, a female employee arrived around 6:00 a.m., to catch up on some work. It felt like someone was already there... but she looked around, and didn't see anyone. She touched her desk, and noticed that it was ice-cold. She thought that perhaps the air conditioner had been left on all night—but the thermometer registered seventy-two degrees. When the woman returned to her desk, it was no longer cold. However, as she sat down, she felt someone come up behind her, and brush against the chair. She turned around quickly, but saw nothing. Ten minutes later, when she looked up, she saw the figure of a woman in a white dress, floating across the room and vanishing through a wall. Hysterical, the poor girl left the office, undoubtedly in search of some living companions!

Another incident happened to one of the ship's new tour guides. She had been working for only two days, when she decided to venture onto the ship by herself for lunch. As she was coming up from B deck, she noticed a very tall, transparent woman, in a passageway down one of the dark, little alcoves. The figure, which had long hair and was wearing a white dress, was standing still, with one hand resting against the wall. This seems to be the same ghost that was seen by the employee in the Mayfair Room. She has been nicknamed "The Lady in White," by those who have seen her.

Paranormal phenomena have also been associated with rooms B-423 and B-421. A paranormal researcher, using dowsing rods, reported that the starboard side, toward the aft deck, was especially hot with such activity.

Not all the paranormal activity takes place below, in the cabins. On one occasion, a party of four had just finished dinner in Sir Winston's Dining Room. They were walking back to their cabins, across the sun deck, when one of the women in the group saw a lady singing to them. The lady walked around a pillar, and disappeared from sight. The woman turned to her companions and said, "Wasn't she beautiful?" But no one else had seen or heard the mysterious "singing lady."

The next event is said to have happened during the war. It involves a popular game known as "chicken," which was played by the men servicing the boiler rooms. The automatic steel doors were pre-set by a timer, to close slowly. The men would see how many times they could get through, without getting caught. A fellow named Harry reportedly made it through only six-and-a-half times. The door slammed shut, cutting

Harry in two. Supposedly, his ghost is still there-haunting Boiler Room One.

MOST HAUNTED SPOTS

"The "Lady in White" seems to roam all over the ship; she is spotted most often on the sun deck.

Several sightings of "a shadow of a man" have been reported by the ship's barbershop. The barbers have seen this shadow with their peripheral vision.

Numerous "cold spots," and the odors of cigar smoke and After-Shave, are noticed all over the ship, even though smoking is prohibited. The ship is plagued with major electrical problems, and its resident ghosts seem to enjoy locking and unlocking the doors. Most of the paranormal activity takes place either on the B deck, in the boiler rooms, or in the pool area, which is located in the dead center of the ship.

The pool area is very haunted; it has several ghosts, as well as an energy vortex. No matter what the crew does to try and dry it up, the bottom of the empty pool remains wet.

We would like to say a special "thank you" to Will, from the Ghost Tour, who was kind enough to take the time to give us all of the ship's history.

TRAVELOGUE

Long Beach, California

Day One: Thursday, June 13, 11:30 p.m.

The RMS Queen Mary is truly majestic, and greatly resembles the Titanic. We could see it from a half-mile away, bathed in the moonlight, with floodlights further illuminating her mast and smokestacks. When we arrived, we took an elevator to reach the hotel's entrance, in the center of the ship, on the fourth level. We were checked in, and then found our way, down a long, narrow, red-carpeted corridor, to Cabin 471, on the B deck.

We were exhausted, from having traveled all day, and, in less than an hour, we decided to call it a night. As I lay in bed, trying to get to sleep, I was overcome by noises that I can't explain: footsteps; tapping; rattling; it sounded like someone was throwing a truck around. It was so loud, I actually thought something was going to come through the ceiling! I also got the feeling that I was being watched: perhaps it was a spirit, or maybe the Lady in White, silently slipping in out of the walls to observe us. Her presence was not negative, but it was rather unnerving to awaken, during a fitful sleep, and have the sensation of eyes watching you from a dark corner. The entire night was very strange, and I was a little scared.

As Maliena started to fall asleep, she began dreaming about the airplane we had just been on. In her dream, she was trying to push the seat-tray back up. It was stuck, and for some reason, it was choking her. She pushed harder and harder, but it wouldn't budge; it was becoming increasingly difficult for her to breathe. I could hear her coughing, and I began to worry. I was ready to jump out of bed and check on her, but she finally woke up—very startled, and gasping for air. She said she felt like her throat was being squeezed, and her chest was being pushed down. My spirit guides had told me, prior to our journey, that many of the ship's ghosts are not happy about the presence of so many living people. This may have been a way for them to express their distaste for us.

Earlier, when we first arrived, I felt cold spots, and had the feeling of disrupted energy—it felt like my equilibrium was being thrown off. This was a very strong feeling, rather like being drunk, and unable to walk a straight line, accompanied by dizziness and the inability to visually focus. I always recognize this type of disruption as being connected with the paranormal. In this case, it could not have been due to the ship's motion, because the ship was not moving. This feeling remained with me throughout our entire three days on board; it was the strongest in our room, in the halls of B deck, and by the pool.

Day Two: Friday, June 14

Early today, Maliena took a walk alone, and found her way to the front of the ship. She was following one of the ship's self-guided tours, and came across a door that should have been shut, but wasn't. She peeked into the pitch-black room, and noticed what looked like a glowing orb. It was very faint, about the size of a tennis ball, and it dissipated quickly. The door led to some sort of an air duct, and the vent sounded like someone's breath; but under that noise, she heard what seemed like the deep breathing of a man. Then the door behind her swung in and bumped her, trying to close. That spooked her enough to leave, and come and get Shante and me. I wasn't quite ready, so the girls departed without me; we agreed to meet in an hour. They returned to the site of the orb. The door was still ajar, but they didn't see anything. There was no orb or heavy breathing, but the air vent was still making that same noise. After we met up, we walked through the endless corridors of the ship, visiting each area, looking through the numerous gift shops, and gazing at the spectacular salons. The most impressive salon was the Queen's salon, which is one of the few areas open to the public. It was the original ballroom, and it gives you a glimpse into the elegance of the day. The majesty of this ballroom is beyond compare. At one end is a grand fireplace, with an Art Deco mural soaring forty feet into the air. At the other end is a stage, with an inlaid, wooden dance floor, large enough to hold a big-band orchestra. Ten-foot-tall alabaster lighting is inset into the support columns. You can easily envision movie-star legends from the1940's, sitting at candlelit tables, sipping cocktails as the big bands played.

Awhile later, I decided to take a self-guided tour of the Queen Mary artifacts. These exhibits also enable you to witness another era. You see actual first-class suites, decorated in the style of the late 1930's. These suites were designed with beautiful Art Deco furnishings, elegant living rooms, and separate bedrooms, with vanity areas for dressing, and electric fireplaces for chilly nights at sea. Truly, these suites were fit for royalty.

After a complete tour of the ship we spent the rest of the afternoon visiting a local graveyard, reputedly haunted, as well as a mausoleum. Both were beautiful, and we took some fantastic photos, but I assure you, neither of them proved to be haunted. I always hear stories about haunted cemeteries, but I find it very rare for ghosts to actually haunt their own graves. It is not very logical to think that a ghost will follow its own corpse to a burial plot, and then stay there for the duration. Because they choose to become ghosts at the moment of death, they may linger where they are killed, due to confusion. But ghosts don't normally follow their physical bodies. Actually, I find the reverse to be true. Usually, ghosts return to places they once lived, like their homes, or, to special places that hold fond memories for them.

June 14, 3:30-6:00 p.m.

We really exhausted ourselves during the day. After spending a few hours in Long Beach, we returned to the ship, where we walked around the different gift shops. When we were planning this trip, none of us realized how much of the ship would be locked, and off-limits. The infamous haunted areas, the pool and boiler rooms are accessible only via guided tours, at ten dollars per person. These tours have been turned into a light hearted Halloween horror show called "Legends and Ghost Tour", complete with overly dramatic tour guides, obnoxious strobe lights, fake steam, and recorded noises.

Although we made several calls to the public relations representative, hoping to gain access to the restricted areas, she was of no help. She wasn't even interested when my assistant told her that I was an author, writing a book about the ghosts aboard. She informed Shanté that we would have had to provide them with a written request in advance, and that these requests take time to process. Obviously, with only one day left, that was not going to happen. So, except for three complimentary tickets to their commercial ghost tour, we were left to our own devices. If you visit the Queen Mary, don't expect too much help from their staff. When we made our reservations, and told them we were coming to investigate ghosts for a forthcoming book, no one mentioned the ship's ghost tour, or the fact that the ship's most haunted areas are closed to the general public, except during these frivolous tours.

The 5:45 p.m. tour was almost the last of the day. We arrived ten minutes early, and were first in line. The only person we found, who seemed passionate about the ship's history, was a man named Will, who trains the employees as guides for the ship's Ghost Tour.

He was happy to relate the ship's history to us, and to recount some of the ghost stories he had heard over the years. He gave us permission to tape record him, and it was very interesting. Then we embarked on the dreaded tour, which has sent "oh so many" toddlers into hysterics.

As we were watching a short documentary film, about the Queen Mary's war efforts and her collection of ghostly inhabitants, I made a conscious effort to open myself up to psychic information. When I sensed that someone was standing right next to me, the hair on my arms stood up. Something touched me: I smelled the strong scent of cigarette smoke, and a cold chill ran through me. I could feel a presence, and I kept looking around to try and see something. Shante also smelled the strong, cigarette odor. The odor lasted about the same length of time it would have taken to actually smoke a cigarette. Psychically, I received a visual of a young man in his twenties. He was wearing a white sailor's uniform, and he was the ghostly presence that had touched me. I acknowledged him, but he didn't seem to want anything other than to observe the surroundings.

The tour guide started to lead the way down a hall that led to the pool. Despite the Hollywood setup, complete with fake spider webs and black lights, the pool still had an ominous feeling about it, and looked exactly as it had on all of the television programs we had watched. And YES, the bottom of the pool really was wet.

We were led to a special, elevated viewing section, which overlooked the empty pool. We spread out evenly along a guardrail, and then, quite dramatically, the guide turned off the lights. Shante was on my left, and Maliena was in the middle. Maliena remembered the notice she had seen outside, and she took one large step backward, so she wouldn't "get wet," as the warning had said. She said it was so dark, that she could barely see either one of us. At almost the same moment as the blackout, I felt a light brush across my back. Instinctively, I thought it was Maliena or Shante, but psychically I also received a vision of a small girl trying to tug on me. I didn't have time to think about it too much. After the guide finished his speech, we witnessed a short light show, and, of course, the water. The lights were turned on, and we were escorted down to the boiler rooms, where the ridiculous "haunting extravaganza" continued.

Fifteen screaming kids nearly knocked us over, as we were herded onto an elevator to descend to Boiler Room One. As soon as we entered, I felt the grief, death, heat, and other horrible conditions, which had filled this room in the past. Many men had died here, not to mention the 300 men from the Curacoa, whose screams no doubt reached the inside of these walls. I was tapping into the imprint of all the horror and loss of life that had occurred.

The Ghost Tour provided us with everything from exploding pipes, to fake water leakage in the bow, to a poor reenactment of the devastation of the HMS Curacoa. There was also a pirate-like hologram of half-hatch Harry, projected onto a transparent screen. That little scare lasted about ten minutes, and then, as quickly as it had begun, it was over. Our frantic and phony tour guide directed us back up the stairwell, and onto the R deck. He left us there—a little wet, very disappointed, and exceedingly agitated, from the three nine-year-old girls who had repeatedly trampled on our feet throughout the tour.

When we returned to our room, we sadly agreed that the tour had made a mockery of the genuine tragedies that had befallen the ship throughout its history. For those under the age of fifteen, it is probably great entertainment. But what bothered me the most, is the unhappiness that these tours cause to the ship's resident ghosts. It is difficult to trivialize so much loss of life; these are not stories to joke about. The death and destruction was so vast and horrible, that these souls are unable to move on. These ghosts are angry and hurt. It is no wonder the employees refuse to venture there alone, or at night. For us, only one good thing resulted from the ghost tour-it was where we had our first ghost encounter!

I told the girls about the ghost, upon our return to the room. At first, I just asked Maliena if she had touched me during our visit to the pool. "No," she said and explained where she had been standing. My eyes widened a little, because even though I had asked, I already knew what her answer would be. As I said before, when the lights were shut off, I had simultaneously felt someone brush the small of my back, down past my buttocks. The touch was light, but enough to catch my attention. Psychically, I felt that it was the ghost of a small girl, maybe seven or eight years old. She was reaching up, as if trying to get my attention.

As soon as I told my story, Shante confessed that she had experienced the same thing at the same time. She said that as soon as the lights went out, she also had felt a slight brush across her lower back and down past her buttocks. At first, she thought it was the man next to her, and she shot him a nasty glance. To her surprise, he was standing next to a woman, and he was completely engrossed in the presentation. In addition, in order to touch both of us at the same time, he would have had to walk past Maliena, and there wasn't enough room to do that. Also, Shante and I were separated by almost two feet. After putting all of this together, any doubts that Shante might have had were gone.

After we got settled, we came up with a plan. We called the front desk to ask for keys to rooms B-423 and 421. Will, the manager of the Ghost Tour, had told us that these were some very hot spots for ghost activity. We were told that B-423 was already occupied, but we did get the key to B-421. At this point, it was still only around 6:30 p.m. As we walked up to get the key card, all three of us smelled the aroma of tobacco. We had smelled it a few times before, but now it was very strong. We were the only people in the hall, except for a woman and two small children, who were just ahead of us. There was no one around "actually" smoking. I was beginning to realize that paranormal smells on the Queen Mary are quite common. The question remains, does this mean that a ghost is nearby?

When we entered B-421, I saw that there was a ghost in the room with us! He was hovering around, and drifting from corner to corner. I was the only one who could actually see him, but the girls both felt him very distinctly. He had died of a heart attack, and this was where he stayed. The room was small, with twin beds. I pointed out which bed he claimed for himself. This man was in the room with us, and I could smell him like a pair of old, smelly socks. His disposition was not particularly appealing, either. He had no sense of time, and was quite content where he was. This ghost simply existed on the ship, in this environment. We felt a thick heaviness in the room, a residual energy, if you will. He did not seem eager to communicate with me, and really could have cared less about our presence. We decided it would be better to wait until later that night, before doing any more investigating.

June 14, 11:45 p.m.

Armed with cameras, audio and video recorders, and a candle, we painstakingly walked down the long corridor of B deck to room 421. Carefully, we opened the door and crept in, wide-eyed and anxious. We saw that nothing was there. In fact, the atmosphere had felt heavier in the afternoon than it did when we returned that night. The man I had sensed earlier was not there. But we had gone all the way back to retrieve the key, so we decided to stay a little longer. We lit the candle, and began to perform a "mini" séance. We spent about half an hour calling in the spirits. Without any luck we decided to move on.

For the next hour or so, we combed the ship for unlocked doors or passages not yet explored. The only thing we did discover was that at the end of B deck, there was a very short stairwell, maybe ten steps or so, leading down to R deck. To the right were double doors, and to the left was a heavy iron door that said "tourist class," which was bolted shut. But the double doors swung open easily, as they were meant to be part of the fire exit. We realized that we had entered the alcove to the Ghost Tour. This was the passageway that we had hoped to find. For a second, we all became very excited, thinking we had found a way in; but the door leading to the actual hallway was also bolted tightly shut.

From there, we walked around and down to where the elevator was, in an attempt to go up to the sun deck. I heard the elevator doors open again, and I turned around to see who it was, since the ship was so quiet that evening. As I looked, I saw the black shadow of a man stepping out of the elevator. He walked past me, and even reflected off the floor. It was so visible, and it happened so fast, that at first I thought it was a living person. I followed, but he disappeared, and then I realized that he was a ghost. When I came back to where the girls were, the elevator came back up and the doors opened and would not shut. For almost five minutes, the doors to the elevator seemed to have a life of their own. They began to playfully open and close, as if someone were standing inside, randomly pushing buttons. When we reentered the elevator, to return to B deck, Shante was the last to get on. As she tried to step in, the elevator doors began to shut on her. Shante's eyes widened and her breath was cut short as she struggled to avoid being crushed. "That was not very nice!" I said to the ghost. He, on the other hand, must have found this quite amusing, because the doors took on a life of their own again, opening and closing part way. This occurred about half a dozen times, before we finally made it back to the lobby floor.

All three of us hurried off, before something else could happen!

Day Three: Saturday, June 15, 9:00 a.m.

This morning, we all woke up feeling frustrated. Our stay on the Queen Mary was coming to an end. We were disappointed, because we had been unable to enter the pool area alone, and had experienced only two brief encounters with ghosts, plus the "brush up" in the dark. We had much higher expectations. We spent the day in Long Beach, shopping for antiques, and buying supplies for the rest of our trip. Returning to the ship around 8:00 p.m., we settled in for the night.

At 11:10 p.m., I dragged Maliena out of bed, to take one last stroll around the ship. Shante opted to get some sleep. Armed with only a camera and each other, Maliena and I ventured back onto B deck. We walked to the bow, to the end of B deck, where you can only go up or down. It was right where we had ended, the night before. To indulge our incessant habit, of attempting to open locked doors, Maliena climbed down the short flight of steps, and went to the double doors. Strangely enough, she couldn't get them to budge. In all fairness, it is possible that she might not have pushed hard enough; but, on the previous night, they had swung open easily. Then she meandered over to the heavy "tourist class" door, expecting it to be locked, as it had been the night before. But a very funny thing happened— it opened right up.

At first, we thought it would be just like the other side. But as Maliena poked her head in, she saw the familiar, fake spider-webs. There were double doors to the right, another one further to the side, and a barrage of items on an L-shaped counter; to the left was another single door. I couldn't believe it: someone, or something, had unlocked a dead-bolted door, and no other person had been around for hours! "Michelle, come here, quick," Maliena whispered, motioning me to follow.

Bingo!! This opened to the off-limits part of the "Ghosts and Legends Tour." We weren't sure exactly where we were, but we were excited! The day before, black lights and strobes had lit everything. Now, with regular lights, it was a bit disorienting. We made a hasty decision to head to the double doors first. We opened them, and timidly began to walk down the hallway. The realization that this was "the tour," began to sink in. More than anything else, I hoped to make it to the pool; I knew it was the most haunted spot, and I kept repeating this to myself, as we inched our way along.

We made it about half way, when suddenly the doors behind us began to rattle noisily. We both freaked out, thinking it was some person about to discover our intrusion. Then it hit us that it might be "a person," but not a living one! We stared at each other, and then back at the door. "What the hell is that?" breathed Maliena. Both sides of the doors banged together, first the left, then the right, then both together. This happened about six times, with quick, swift raps, like someone was trying to get our attention. We were afraid to move, because if we had angered a ghost, to do so might prove dangerous. Then again, in order to go back, we would have to open the possessed doors! The suspense mounted, as we stood solidly in our tracks, wishing the noise would stop.

Finally, we lost our nerve, and ran back out into the stairwell...well, O.K...it was more like we sprinted. Outside the second door, we paused for a moment to think about what was happening. For two days, we had tried desperately to get someone to let us into the pool area, and our efforts had been unsuccessful. Now, on our very last day, the ghosts themselves had decided to let us in. The doors are never left unlocked, and several employees had told us that the ghosts on the ship were in the habit of locking and unlocking doors as they saw fit. I suppose, in a way, it was the ghosts' gift to us. I wanted to go back and get Shante, so she wouldn't miss this experience, but Maliena was insistent that we shouldn't take the chance of leaving, and not being able to get back in. As much as I wanted Shante to be there, I finally agreed. We knew this would be our last opportunity to explore, so with new resolve, we took some deep breaths and once again opened the tourist class door. We walked through the door on the left, and it brought us to Boiler Room One. From high above, we looked down at the huge, open space. It was amazing: the quiet emptiness was eerie, and far more frightening than anything we had experienced on the official tour. We took a picture of the staircase leading down, as proof that we really were there, and of the big, neon sign on the black-painted stairwell, reading "GREY GHOST WALKWAY." That is when it actually hit us: "Oh my God, we're in!" Two fears began to take shape, which neither of us had anticipated. First, as much as I wanted to wander through these spacious rooms— snapping pictures and inviting a ghost or two for a late-night chat, we were nervous about being caught by any surveillance cameras. Second, and perhaps more likely, was the possibility that an employee might discover the door unlocked, and would re-lock it. Thus we would be stuck, in our pajamas, with only a camera flash to aid us, in a cold, dark, enormous boiler room which had been host to more than a few deaths. Our hearts were fluttering. This room, by far, was the most frightening. The sheer size of it, with its dark steel walls dropping to the bottom of the ship, made us feel tiny and chilled. I could sense a ghostly presence, which was not happy to see us, hiding in a dark corner, its alert eyes observing us with a little less than hate. I didn't need my guides to warn me that it was time to go. My instinctual alarms all went off at once: this place was dangerous. Suffice it to say, we left the boiler room and headed back to the double doors. When I emerged, relief washed over me. I must admit, despite all of my previous paranormal experiences, I was totally freaked by the enormous velocity of the energy that I felt in this boiler room.

Maliena and I felt pulled toward the pool area, anyway. We knew it was off to the right, just not specifically where. So we entered the hall once again, and began to make our way down. This time, the first set of double doors was silent. I veered towards another door, and poked my head in. This was where we had watched the video, the day before, and I knew we were close. A second later, Maliena called, "Michelle, hurry, hurry— I found the pool!" I ran down to the end of the hall, and opened the doors: and there it was—the infamous pool.

I felt like an archaeologist discovering some hidden, never previously opened tomb. It was quite exhilarating, especially because we were "breaking the rules," and venturing into an area not deemed safe enough for the general public. In fact, most of the employees would not even enter this area alone. The pool felt like a huge vortex of energy. We snapped as much film as we could, but unfortunately we only had about four pictures left. We hadn't expected to get in, and didn't have another roll of film. We looked around, trying to absorb as much as possible. The room was large and square, with a walkway going all the way around the pool; staircases along each side came together and dramatically led down to the bottom floor. We could see the entryway to the shower room, chairs and various windows. The pool was enormous and very deep. It had no shallow end, nor did it provide siderailings to help you pull yourself out. Basically, it was an aquatic trap. Along the bottom of the light blue cement, you could see the glistening slickness of water, which apparently was always present-nothing had ever worked to remove it. The moment I walked into the room, it felt like several different spirits tried to attack me. They all hovered around, making me feel claustrophobic. I also felt that a few of them were attempting to enter my body to try and communicate. This is called "trance channeling," when a spirit enters the mediums body and speaks through them. The channel has no way of controlling their body during this time. Some people will speak in a different voice or accent; they can't remember what they say or how much time has passed. You literally share your body with another entity, almost like a possession, but the spirit only stays with you long enough to convey its messages. I do not normally channel in this manner, so this frightened me. It was an invasion of my personal space. Ghosts were hovering all around us, passing in and out of my psychic vision.

My face and chest began to heat up from all the paranormal activity: I turned bright red; I felt like I would spontaneously combust; my stomach began to cramp; and my hands were shaking violently. I couldn't repress the overwhelming feeling of a presence trying to invade my body. I felt bombarded; all I wanted to do was get out of there. Being a sensitive, it's not uncommon for me to temporarily take on physical ailments, emotions, or even traits from the people for whom I read. This had occurred so instantaneously, however, that we were both shocked. Maliena became very nervous, and said she could see the red creeping into my face, getting deeper every second that we stood there. Several times, her eyes darted from me to the door, before she finally said, "Let's go, it's too risky!" But I needed another moment to try and get as much information as possible. This is what happened: we both felt the presence of a fairly young woman, with medium-length, dirty blonde hair, as well as that of a very young girl, with curly blonde hair and a fluffy bow on top of her head. We both saw the same mental picture, although the spirits had not actually manifested. I also detected a young, dark-haired boy. He was very shy, and he stood close to the little girl. At this point, we started to feel skittish, and opted to leave before we were discovered...or possessed!

We ran from the pool area, going up the hall, out the double doors, and through the tourist class door. I walked directly up the stairs, and stopped at the very top to catch my breath. Maliena was behind me. She walked about three-quarters of the way up and also stopped. We were quiet for a moment, contemplating our next move.

Within in a minute, two nicely dressed men walked by, obviously doing what we had done earlier—snooping. We stayed put, as they walked down the stairs and tried the doors to the right. Now remember, this part of the ship was quiet, no one else was around, and the heavy steel doors make a lot of noise when opened and closed. The men tried the doors to the right, but the doors wouldn't budge; the metal made a loud rattling noise that echoed through the corridor. As they started back up the stairs, Maliena sheepishly told them that the other door was open. She smiled broadly at the secret she had let them in on. As we looked at each other, the men turned to us, puzzled. "Do you mean this door?" one of them asked, as he jiggled the handle. We were stupefied: not only was the door we had just come through tightly shut, it was also locked and dead-bolted. We hadn't heard anything—no footsteps on the solid concrete floor, no noise of the door shutting, no locks clicking-nothing! I was so astonished that I ran down and tried the door myself. It was tightly locked. "No way," we said. "We swear, it was not locked a second ago. How could anyone possibly lock it without us hearing? There's just no way!" The men chuckled at us and walked off, not believing it for a second. Interestingly, when we tried the doors to the right, they were now unlocked and opened easily. It was quite evident that the same ghosts who had graciously let us in, had now decided they'd had enough visitors for the night and silently locked the door behind us.

We looked around a bit more, and then headed back to the cabin. We excitedly woke Shante, and repeated our tale. The channeling I had done in the pool and the symptoms I had taken on earlier had left me exhausted. I lay down to try and rest, and a little later Maliena went out into the hall, to log everything while it was still fresh in her mind. Afterwards, she still couldn't sleep, so she decided to do one last walk-through. It was now around 2:00 a.m. Being the little skeptic that she is, she decided to call Security on the house phone, when she was half way down the hall to R deck, to find out when the cleaning staff had left that day. Security verified that they had left by 9:00 p.m. This proved that no human had been down in that area of the ship, who could have unlocked and then relocked the doors. So, it had to have been the ghosts! The crewmember that she spoke to, laughed at her and said, "Don't you know this ship is haunted?" She then proceeded to tell Maliena that doors on the ship were known to lock and unlock themselves, almost on a daily basis. She also tried to see if she could get someone to take us back to that section of the ship. But the crew was too frightened, and no one was willing to venture down there so late at night.

We found out later why we had such a difficult time getting the ship's employees to cooperate with our investigation. Although we cannot mention names or positions, we found one other staff member who was willing to speak to us about the happenings on the ship. Apparently, the crew had been a bit edgy during our visit, because of a paranormal incident that had taken place about a week before our arrival. Two maids had been getting one of the salons ready for a party, or a convention of some sort. One of them noticed a chair in the middle of the room, with a mannequin sitting on it. Because they could only see the back of it, they thought it was a real person. They walked over, and tapped its shoulder, then realized it was a fake. But they were puzzled as to how it had ended up in the salon to begin with, and figured it must have been from one of the ship's storage compartments. Before they could pick it up, the head of the mannequin spun around to face them, and its eyelids snapped open. A disembodied voice queried, "So, when does the party start?" Both maids ran out, screaming for help. Another crewmember nearby went back in to examine the mannequin, but found nothing. There was no phony gag tape inside, or anything else that would prove it a hoax. With no explanation for the manifestation, everyone was left feeling very nervous. Obviously, among other things, these ghosts have a sense of humor!

CHANNELED INFORMATION

Although I didn't see as many apparitions as I had hoped, I did receive a lot of channeled information. I decided that the best way to relay this to you would be to write a separate "channeled section," for each location we visited. During our three-day stay at the Queen Mary, this is what I learned from the spirits that reside there, as well as from my own guides and angels.

The enormous pool was constructed in the 1930's; there is no shallow end, or ladders along the sides, making it difficult to climb out. One wrong move could prove fatal, and, for several people, it did. Upon entering the pool area, I felt the presence of many spirits, but what I also felt was an awesome and powerful vortex. This vortex is actually inside the pool, and its swirling energy creates a dizzying effect. Ghosts flow in and out of it to the astral realms. The vortex energizes the area, as well as those entities near it. So, if you are unable to feel the ghosts, you will definitely feel the vortex.

There are three resident ghosts who dwell in the pool area; the energy level is unbelievable, and comes at you the minute you enter the room. The strongest ghost is the little girl. Her name is Claudia. She wears a pastel, calico-print party dress, with a hem that goes below her knees. She has lots of petticoats, lace bobby socks, and shiny, white, patent leather shoes. Her blonde hair is worn in ringlets, and a portion of it is tied with a big floppy bow, matching her dress. At the time of her physical death, she was about eight years old. She is very mischievous, and spends much of her time skipping and playing around the pool. It is likely that she wandered off during a party she was attending with her parents, and she wound up in the pool area. Since the pool has no ledges or rails, it was easy for her to slip and fall in. The weight of her dress and shoes alone would have bogged her down considerably. She probably didn't have enough upper-body strength to pull herself out, and, in fact, if the water level was at all low, her arms were probably too short to allow her to reach up and grab the sides. After a short time of trying to keep afloat, her strength gone, she simply drowned. Earlier in the day, when Shante and I had felt our backs being touched, this was the spirit responsible. Claudia and the little boy are also the ones who unlocked the door for us on our last night. I've noticed, through my experiences, that many children become wayward, when they die tragically. Through prayer and meditation, I have been given a simple reason for this: many such children do not understand what has happened, and they don't realize that they are dead. This is also why many ghosts, who actually interact with the living, are children. They have a childish mentality, and, even though their angels and guides come to help them, they often refuse out of fear or confusion.

The second spirit I saw was that of the small, shy boy, mentioned earlier. His energy is not very strong. He plays with the little girl, but hides from people. He has pale skin, dark hair and blue eyes; he shows himself with knickers, and a dinner jacket with a white fluffy shirt underneath. He is always with the little girl, who looks out for him, but she is more charismatic. The circumstances of his death were not made clear to me, but he is from the same era as the little girl.

The third spirit was that of a young woman in her mid-twenties, named Jane. She wore a plain, 1940's style swimsuit, the one-piece kind that came down to the upper thigh, with crisscross straps in the back. She also wore a tight-fitting, rubber swim cap, to cover her hair. Both Maliena and I received this image. Later, after comparing notes, we realized it was the same spirit. She was fairly tall, for a woman of that time, with broad shoulders. She was an excellent swimmer, and enjoyed this activity daily. It may even have been her career. I also picked up the image that the pool's slide had originally been a diving board. Jane's love for swimming is what still attracts her to the pool. She always preferred to swim alone, and would wait until everyone had gone before going into the water herself. One evening, while diving into the pool, she hit her head, was knocked unconscious, and drowned. The tragedy is that if someone else had been there, she would have been saved. After Jane's death, the diving board was probably removed, and replaced with a slide. Jane remains in the pool, almost unaware of the living. She spends her time swimming leisurely, or doing laps. Jane is the ghost responsible for keeping the bottom of the pool wet.

The other spirits we encountered during our stay also provided much historic information. The solider that manifested during the documentary told a tragic tale of pain and despair. The Queen Mary had picked him up during the war, when he was badly wounded. Because the ship was so crowded, he was left on the sun deck, and there he died. His premature death, his fear, and the shock from his injuries and what he had seen in battle, caused him to continue to live with that despair, even after he died. The solider is an observer; he wanders the sun deck, and the lower floors. I also was made aware of a ghost in the boiler rooms; he is not the only one there, but he is definitely one of the strongest. In life, he had been on the ship during the war. He was a big, muscular man, with a very hard exterior, who had gotten used to the heat and hard labor of the boiler rooms. He ran the show, oversaw the men, and kept a close eye on the boilers. He was a bit ignorant, very stern, and he didn't believe in God. The only thing he knew how to do well, was his job on the ship. In a horrible explosion, which killed several men, he tried to save those that he could. He ended up taking the brunt of it himself, and he died as well. Now he remains in Boiler Room One, skulking around and disapproving of the ship's current status. In fact, he is so unhappy with the changes, that he often moans loudly, and clangs a large wrench on the metal. Most of the employees, who refuse to go down there alone, have this ghost to thank. He is the dark, ominous force that makes your skin crawl and the hair on your neck prickle up. His were the penetrating eyes we saw, the night before we left. He considers it unforgivable that the Ghost Tour has made a mockery of his life's story.

There is also the black shadow that I saw in the elevator-a ghost reportedly seen by others. He was a shopkeeper, sometime during the late 1950's, who worked and lived on the ship. I could not receive any information about why he still remains here; I was only told that he likes to roam the upper decks and observe different people as they come and go. Unlike Jane, he is fully aware of the ship's changing times and people. He seems almost indifferent—neither happy nor angry— but he does amuse himself with the occasional prank.

I estimate that, at one time, as many as twenty ghosts made the Queen Mary their home; right now, about ten of them are still on board. Because so many ghosts are from different time periods, they recreate their own versions of the ship. It's as if the ship has layers of different time periods, and in each layer, different ghosts roam. As I channeled this, I gained some new insight about ghosts. Something I did not know, but was told, is that when there are many ghosts in one area, there can be a kind of seniority. In the case of the Queen Mary, there is a "head ghost." The Lady in White is the oldest ghost, and she has the run of the ship. I was able to channel an enormous amount of information about this ghost. Her name is Mary, and she was a wealthy, first-class passenger who boarded the ship in the late 1930's, with a female attendant who was her confidant. Mary was an average-looking, middle-aged woman, with a medium build and sandy brown hair, who dressed in the finest fashions. In life, Mary was very ill. She suffered from a chronic lung disorder, which kept her social activities very limited. She was very lonely, despite the fact that she was educated and wealthy. When she planned her trip, Mary made the decision that this one would be different. No matter what the cost, she was embarking on an adventure. This was her opportunity to live the life that she had longed for, one full of ongoing parties with aristocratic society from all over the world. She was going to dine out for every meal, and wear beautiful formal clothes for dinner and dancing. Mary knew that pushing herself with constant activities would further risk her failing health, but she didn't care. She stayed on A deck with her assistant, and fell in love with the grandeur of the ship. Unfortunately, her adventure cost her the ultimate price: her life. She died from fluid on the lungs.

At the time of her death, she was very angry with God. So, when she finally passed over and saw herself in a lighter form, she looked and felt remarkably well. It was then that she decided to stay on the ship. The Lady in White is the oldest resident ghost, and in a way, she calls the shots. When she does show herself, her apparition wears a beautiful, flowing, floor-length, white gown. That's really what we see, more than any facial features. She loves the excitement of the Queen Mary, and enjoys trying to interact with people. However, like most of the ghosts on board, she doesn't like the renovations. As head ghost, she encourages the other ghosts to show their displeasure by causing the electrical appliances to malfunction, making noises, and messing things up which have already been tidied. Mary is the ghost that was responsible for the electrical problems on B deck, when some of the rooms were renovated into offices. For now, Mary (or "The Lady in White," as we have come to know her), is content to roam the ship, and enjoy all of the things that she lacked in life.

Most of the ghosts prefer to stay in their favorite areas, like the woman at the pool. I do not believe that they interact with each other, unless they are in the same reality. By that, I mean that each ghost is willingly living their afterlife as they please. Some stay in the era they died, and with their thoughts, they actively create the scenario that they wish to experience. For example, the three strong spirits in the pool are able to interact with each other and instantly manifest their reality, but when other spirits wander into the pool, they don't see each other. Why? Because other spirits in other time dimensions are not a part of their reality.

The spirits in the boiler room are very upset by the ship's ghost tours. They think these tours make fun of them, and show disrespect. These men served their country with honor, and their pride and dignity have been hurt. In this portion of the ship, you can feel their eyes upon you; they bang around in the quiet of the night, hoping any humans in their vicinity will get scared and leave. These guys are unhappy, but they probably wouldn't injure anyone.

At the bottom of the boat, there was a time when the collision with the Curacoa was an energy imprint, but it has faded over the years. Even though it still carries tremendously cumbersome energy, the scene is no longer repeating itself. More than anything, as you leave the bow of the boat, the Curacoa's imprint, far below the water line, causes one to feel sad and lonely.

Sunday, June 16, 10:00 a.m.

We woke up this morning with a renewed sense of adventure. We finished our packing, and decided, as a farewell treat, to indulge in one of the Queen Mary's time-honored traditions: Sunday Brunch. In the manner of years gone by, we made our way to the ballroom. As we stood waiting in line, you could feel the anticipation. A smiling waiter greeted us with champagne, and freshly squeezed orange juice; the separate buffet tables were decorated with magnificent, towering ice sculptures; and the food was absolutely delicious.

We dined leisurely, and discussed our plans for the day. Then we packed up our sports utility vehicle, and headed to our next destination. From Long Beach, we drove through Death Valley. This name alone elicits visions of a long ride, through flat, desolate land. But this proved not to be true. After only a short ride, through a desert strangely without cactus, we came to a mountain pass. Our SUV labored uphill. My foot was pressing the gas pedal to the floor, but we couldn't reach a speed of over fifty miles an hour. At this rate, we would never arrive on schedule at our next haunted site. Weaving our way to the top, we found ourselves traveling on a narrow, steep mountain road, that had no guardrails. It was as if we were on "Mother Nature's Roller Coaster Ride." We picked up some speed, as we drove down the two-lane mountain road. The landscape was fascinating. Our vehicle's temperature gage read one hundred degrees, as we trekked on. The scorching heat of the sun, and the quiet of the surrounding land, allowed us to reflect on what had transpired in the last three days, as well as what might be awaiting us, on the other side of this seemingly endless terrain.

For life in the present
there is no death!
Death is not an event in this life,
it is a fact in this world

— Wittgenstein

CHAPTER

4

THE GOLDFIELD HOTEL
GOLDFIELD, NEVADA

HOTEL HISTORY

*G*oldfield, Nevada was founded in 1902. By 1907, it had become the largest town in the state, with a population of thirty thousand. Goldfield's boom year was 1906, when its local mines produced eleven million dollars in gold.

George Winfield was the original owner of the Goldfield Hotel, which opened in 1908 with 154 rooms. The hotel burned down, sometime during the 1920's, and was rebuilt, shortly thereafter. The hotel was closed for several years, after George Winfield died. Many years later, a millionaire purchased the hotel, and poured tons of money into its renovations. Eventually, he went bankrupt, and the building was left in disrepair. To this day, the hotel is plagued with electrical and plumbing problems (including an elevator shaft that fills with water, no matter how many times it is drained), which have prevented it from reopening. In addition, a huge amount of back taxes are owed on the property, which is presently under state control. The County Commissioner's office gave us permission to enter the Goldfield and investigate its hauntings.

Over the years, several deaths have reportedly occurred in the building. There have been murders, as well as accidental deaths caused by the building's dilapidated condition.

HAUNTED HISTORY

There is very little documented information about the participants of the hotel's hauntings. The only historical facts we could find were documents stating that the original owner was George Winfield.

Two versions of a grisly story are told about the Goldfield's past. The first is that George Winfield impregnated a prostitute named Elizabeth. When George discovered Elizabeth's "embarrassing condition," he locked her in Room 109, and chained her to a radiator. When she gave birth George reportedly threw the newborn down one of the old mineshafts in the basement, Elizabeth died soon after. Cause of death-unknown!

The second story is almost identical to the first, except that Elizabeth is said to be Winfield's daughter.

She was pregnant and unwed, and he was trying to cover up her indiscretion.

From various sources, I have uncovered the following information regarding the Goldfield's hauntings: The ghost of Elizabeth is said to haunt Room 109, the room where she was locked during her pregnancy, and chained to the radiator. Her ghost has been seen floating through the hotel, still pregnant and dressed in a white nightgown. A reporter from Las Vegas photographed the radiator in Room 109. When he developed the film, Elizabeth's image appeared hovering above the radiator, in the picture of a room that was supposedly empty.

The ghost of George Winfield is also said to haunt the hotel. He was a cigar smoker during life, and, still to this day people have reported a cigar-smoke odor, still lingering in the hotel's halls. In another incident, fresh cigar ash was found inside a fuse box, which had not been opened for fifty years. At times, a dark shadow will manifest for people to see: perhaps this is the silhouette of George himself! The Gold Room has been noted for a ghost that stabs people, although we were unable to verify this.

A midget and two small children have been seen and felt at the bottom of the main staircase, and a baby's cries have been heard on lonely nights.

Many psychics say that the hotel is sitting on one of the seven portals to the other side.

MOST HAUNTED SPOTS

Room 109; the George Winfield Room; the Gold Room; the staircase.

TRAVELOGUE

Sunday, June 16, evening

We arrived in Goldfield around 7:30 p.m. The first thing we did was drive around to get a feel for the place. The hotel is in the dead center of a tiny, mining town. Goldfield looks like a lived-in ghost town: once-thriving businesses are boarded with plywood signs, saying "Closed," in red spray paint. We drove around the outside of the immense hotel, then proceeded to the front to see if there was a door that would open. We were hoping to look around while it was still daylight, so we could get our bearings. But the hotel was securely locked. Maliena managed to squeeze through a chain-link fence, and go down an outside stairwell, where she felt an ice-cold breeze, coming from the basement. But the only other living creature we saw was a wild-eyed tabby cat, behind the hotel.

We got back into our truck and continued on. Everything was closed, except for the County Commissioner's office and the police station. There was only one working payphone in the entire town, not even a grocery store had been able to survive. We called our contact person, but no one was home, so we went to the police station to check in, and see if they could locate the hotel keys for us. Shante went in alone while Maliena and I waited in the car. The only fellow at the station was the dispatcher, who seemed surprisingly young to live in a desolate town like this. He was kind enough to make a few phone calls, to see who had the keys. As we waited for the police chief to call back, Shante asked him if he had always lived here. He answered that he had moved from San Francisco. "Why would you choose to move to a town like this?" she asked, out of curiosity. "Well, to tell you the truth," he said, matter-of-factly, "they offer two free burial plots as an incentive to move into this county." This answer was as dark and bizarre as the town itself. Just then, the phone rang. The dispatcher was told that our contact from the County Commissioner's office was the only one with keys to the hotel. We were back to square one.

Finally, we gave up, and headed out to Tonopah, where we had a hotel room reserved for the night. We rested, and prepared our equipment, as we waited for the phone call giving us the go ahead. About 9:30 p.m., we heard from the women who were going to escort us. We made plans to meet them in front of the Goldfield, at 11:30 p.m. This time, we were armed with our equipment: flashlights, camera, video, audio, and extra batteries.

When we arrived, two women from the Commissioner's office (we'll call them Gwen and Pat) greeted us. They had permission to let us into the building, and they decided to join our ghost expedition. Gwen put the key into the lock, but it would not work. She made an emergency call to maintenance personnel, and a big man soon appeared, blurry-eyed but friendly, to open the building's door.

It was now past midnight. The moment we entered, strange things began to happen. First, as we walked inside, the door slammed behind us—not slow and creaking, but hard and fast, like someone had grabbed the handle and flung it shut. The glass in the doors vibrated dangerously. Right away, we were caught off-guard, and we jumped and then froze in our tracks. The air around us felt thick, and lifeless. No one breathed, as we gazed around the hotel's dark interior. Without electricity, our flashlights were our only source of light to see into the shadowy recesses. Slowly, we composed ourselves, and ventured further inside. I felt a hollow, intense energy all around us. This hotel supplied a massive vortex that was powerful in nature, allowing spirits to travel in and out at different times. I felt the surging energy even before I stepped across the threshold, but now I was flooded with an icy feeling, as the vortex spun around us. I knew we had to be very cautious, because the front door was only a taste of what was to come.

Directly inside the lobby, was a long, front desk, standing in front of an ancient elevator. To the right of the desk was a staircase, curling up around the elevator. Also in the lobby, was an old, upright piano, and a six-foot tall safe, built into the back wall. To the far right of the desk, there were two large gathering rooms, stacked with lumber, and miscellaneous building materials. From the second room, a long hallway extends back to the first-floor bedrooms, including Room 109. All of the floors were wood, and the interior of the building gave me the impression that it should have been condemned. To the left of the front desk was another larger room, maybe the Gold Room. At the rear of that room, a staircase descended to the basement. The stone and cement basement was a maze in itself. It contains mineshafts, elevator machinery, food pantries, and rooms that had been once used as shops. Earlier that day, when Maliena snuck down the outside stairwell, she felt an ice-cold breeze coming from what we thought was a mineshaft. But one of the women from the Commissioner's office assured us that the shafts had been completely sealed, years ago. This was a strong confirmation to me that the cold air was coming from the vortex, which seemed to swirl around in the building, pulsating sporadically. We also knew that one of those shafts was the dark abyss into which Elizabeth's baby had been thrown.

We first ascended the stairs by the front desk, and found sleeping rooms on three more levels. Each level had a long, horizontal hall, with the stairs and elevator running through the middle, and another hallway running vertically, at the end of each side.

After we got our bearings, we lit some candles on the front desk, and set up our video camera facing the stairwell that was reported to be very haunted. We had decided to start our investigation by going to the right, toward Elizabeth's room, but before I could head that way, something touched my back. It was just a wispy brush, but well defined. A cold sensation flooded over me, and I knew it had to be the ghost of George! I shuddered at my first encounter, and tried, unsuccessfully, to shake off the icy feeling George's ghost had left on me.

The first room on this floor was a large, open space,

filled with the clutter of old boards, paint buckets and a variety of unused tools. The room probably had been a bar, or maybe even the dining room. The swirling energy from the vortex was black and gray, and seemed to cast dark shadows on the walls as we walked by. We reached the hall, which went up two or three stairs to reveal rooms on either side. I felt that these rooms were for chambermaids, and other live-in employees, such as cooks, barkeepers, maids, etc. Each room on this floor was very small, containing a tiny bathroom and closet. All of the doors had been removed, and the numbers were not in proper sequence, but we were able to find what we were looking for—the second door to the left, which still had a rusted radiator in the corner.

After doing some quick math, and from the heavy, sad energy, I knew this had to be 109. Almost immediately, everyone's equilibrium was thrown off. One spot in particular was so powerful that I had to grab the wall for extra support. An eerie presence seemed to envelop the room, and there were several cold spots. We left 109 and continued down the hall, but we didn't really feel very much, so we headed back to the main entryway.

When we returned to the lobby, we were surprised to find that the front door was now wide open. The night air was still and pleasant, yet somehow the door was pushed open, despite the fact that it had been latched shut. One of the girls said, "How could the wind shut and then open the same door?" The answer was, "It didn't!" The wind had nothing to do with the door; the only explanation was a paranormal one. To humor us, Gwen found a heavy, yellow, industrial-sized mop bucket, which she pushed in front of the door, after we shut it. Once again, we began to climb the dark, creaky stairs.

We walked up around ten steps to a small square landing, and then another ten steps that wound around the elevator shaft to the second-floor hallway. I felt like someone was following right behind me. I could feel his eyes on me, and I received a vision of a man with his hands reaching over to grab my shoulders. But even worse, I could feel his horrible, cold breath on the back of my neck, making my hair rise. I stopped for a moment, and tried to shrug the feeling off, but this ghost wouldn't leave me alone. There was a strong smell of cigar, or sweet tobacco. The entire group could smell it. There were several cold spots in this musty building, especially near the elevator, where the temperature was absolutely freezing. The energy on the second floor, which was caused by the vortex and George was by far the strongest, and the air was like ice. Even more interesting, was that the middle of the vortex contained a separate portal. Entities were coming in and out of this portal, which is an actual doorway into other dimensions: this is very rare, and very dangerous.

George and Elizabeth do not travel outside of the hotel, nor do they interact with other spirits. None-the-less other spirits are there at times. Several of us saw dark shadows with our peripheral vision. One of these shadows was in a doorway, silhouetted from the moonlight spilling in from a window. The silhouette wavered, faintly fading in and out. I also saw a glowing orb about 15 feet away next to one of the hotel room doors. I am fairly certain that the orb had something to do with the energy of the portal only a few feet away. I couldn't quite make out who, it was. I kept pointing it out to the other girls, but only one other person noticed it. As I concentrated on the orb, I saw George's shadow step out from one of the doorways, revealing to me his side profile. As soon as I focused, his profile dissolved. The five of us became increasingly nervous, and we found ourselves huddling a bit closer together.

An extra large suite with a balcony was directly opposite the second-floor elevator. I felt George's presence very strongly in this room. He seemed to be toying with us; he wouldn't come out and show himself, but was content to dance in the shadows and play little tricks. I mentioned to the group that this was his favorite area of the hotel. In life, he would hang out in this suite, which faces the front of the hotel. He would walk out onto the balcony, smoking his big cigar, and watch the people going up and down the busy street. On the balcony, he could wave, or call out to some of his friends, which made him feel very important.

As we examined the elevator, Gwen said, "Oh, go in if you want, it's still a working elevator." We laughed a bit uneasily, and declined the invitation. Ironically, Maliena told me, weeks before our trip, that she dreamt of an elevator that we got into, it fell fast and crashed into a basement once we stepped inside. She saw herself die. This dream was a premonition—a warning not to get into this elevator. Later, Maliena told me that when Gwen asked if we wanted to step inside the elevator, she experienced déjà vu. It was as if her dream were recurring, only this time she was awake!

We continued our climb, up the remaining three levels. The higher we went, the hotter it got. The air was absolutely stifling. As we ascended to the fourth level, Maliena ran out of film, and had to return to the lobby for her camera bag. The trip down was uneventful, but she confessed that it was spooky, to be alone in the dark. As she began to walk back upstairs, she had the feeling that someone was right behind her, almost mimicking her footsteps. She stopped three different times, and quickly turned to point her flashlight in every direction, but she never saw anything. As she continued up, dark shadows started to bounce along with her, creating a frightful vision. The faster she walked, the bolder these dark images became; they leered at her, in a menacing fashion. She was overcome by a sudden urge to run up the remaining flight, but just before she did, she looked down at the stairs and noticed a large hole in the middle of the third step. Too much pressure could have sent her straight through! The thought of falling four stories, to a possible grizzly death, was more than enough incentive for her to remain at a steady walk. Despite her growing panic, Maliena swallowed hard and continued on... slowly! She met up with us, as we were returning to the third level. Her face was pale, and beads of sweat stood out on her forehead, as she explained what had just happened. This confirmed what I already knew: George was evil and malicious; he was not just observing us, he was trying to scare us away!

As we debated our next move, all five of us heard a very distinct, tortured, disembodied cry. We were stunned. At first it was loud and clear, but then all became silent. I can only describe the wail as definitely female, hollow, and agonizing. I knew it was coming from the downstairs, somewhere near Room 109. No human could mimic the sound that Elizabeth had just made. I knew it was she, and my heart ached for this lost soul, too frightened of her tormentor to reveal herself.

We waited with baited breath, to see if she would call out again, but there was nothing. We reviewed our audio and videotapes, but neither device had picked up her loud cry, even though both recorders were sensitive enough to pick up passing trucks from the street.

We decided to head back down to the basement, to see what we could find. On the ground floor, we picked up our thermometer to try and measure any paranormal interference we might get. We walked through the side room on the left, which looked like it had recently been used as a meeting room, and headed for the stairwell at the back. The thermometer read 70 degrees. As we descended the long flight of stairs into the basement area, we felt the temperature began to drop; yet the thermometer began to rise. In fact, in less then five minutes, the reading went from 70 to 95 degrees. But it was freezing cold. This flux was caused by a combination of paranormal interference to our device, plus the intense energy from the vortex.

One of the first areas we looked through was a large space with a boarded-up mineshaft and the old, original, elevator mechanism. This was also the room where I felt that Elizabeth's baby had died. The baby is not a ghost, as it is rumored to be, but in fact is an energy imprint. The cries that people hear late at night are not coming from a ghostly baby floating around, but from the residual energy that the atrocity of the infant's murder left behind. What happened was so horrific, that it left a very heavy imprint in the room. It is destined to keep repeating itself, until it fades out. The moment the baby was thrown down the mineshaft, the soul left its tiny body and transcended back to the heavens. The soul of the infant is not haunting the hotel.

Elizabeth is unable to deal with her grief and loss, and it is easier for her to imagine that her child has not yet been born. That is why, when she does manifest, she appears to be pregnant. You must remember that a wayward spirit has the ability to create these things just by believing in them. Many ghosts will recreate the way their homes looked, the people they were bonded to, or even their previous physical features.

As we moved on from this area, we realized that the basement was filled with different rooms and hallways. Cobwebs were everywhere, along with old machinery that no longer worked; there was cold spot, after cold spot, and areas where we felt dizzy and off balance.

We split up, and each of us explored on our own. Maliena was walking down the hall, when she discovered a small, concrete room, maybe six-foot-by-six. She peered in, and it seemed to be empty, about the size of a large closet, only square. She stood there for a moment, wondering if she should go in. She looked down at her shoes, and saw fresh, rust-colored mud all over them. She reached down and touched the floor, ending up with gross goo on her fingers: her attempt to wipe them off on the wall, made an even bigger mess. The goo seemed to be more like clay, than mud. At this point, the rest of us caught up with her, and we peered into the room to start examining it.

Maliena decided to have a closer look, to try and figure out what had leaked onto the concrete floor. She took a step forward, but before she could put her foot down, she realized that it wasn't wet concrete at all—it was water! This wasn't a room, but the service elevator shaft-the one always filled with water, which no one could ever drain. Floating on top of the water were ore deposits, making it look very much like wet concrete. Grateful to have avoided that disaster, we were all quite ready to leave the basement. There was no telling how deep that water was. In fact, as we turned to leave Gwen tossed a stone into the water, we waited breathlessly but there was no sound of it hitting the bottom, it seemed endless! Had she fallen in, she could have been in serious trouble.

We began to ascend the stairs, in single file. I was in the middle, and when I reached the first landing, I let out a little yelp, as something tried to push me back down the stairs. It felt like someone grabbed the tip of my shoe and pushed up on it, as I tried to put my foot down. It created a springboard effect, and I clumsily took a step backward. I didn't see anything and there was no explanation for my loss of balance, because my footing was stable. From behind me, Maliena said it appeared as if some unseen person had shoved me. We got back to the top of the stairs and walked into the main lobby, hoping for a minute to catch our breath.

Much to our surprise, the door had been opened again: the bucket we placed in front of it had been pushed out of the way. Gwen kept saying she thought it was the wind. However, there was only a gentle breeze that night. Even a strong gust of wind would most likely not have been able to unlatch and open the heavy front door, and push the mop bucket that far away. Also, our three votive candles on the front desk were still burning; if it had been the wind, the candles would have blown out, or at least spilled a little wax-but they were untouched. The first time, the door had been shut by an unseen force, and then later opened. It's not likely that the wind would be responsible for both opening and closing the door. After a short debate, four out of five of us agreed that it was another of George's antics.

At this point, we took about a fifteen-minute break, and sat outside on the front porch. The night was lovely and calm, and overhead, the stars were shining brightly.

But the Goldfield Hotel made an incredibly ominous backdrop, for this quiet peaceful scene. We decided to go back for one more walk-through, hoping for a last-minute manifestation.

I returned to Room 109, with two of the other girls. At some point, I started to get a throbbing, aching pain in my right leg. I had a vision of Elizabeth, and her leg was badly hurt. It was the same leg that was chained to the radiator. As we reached her room, I began to really pick up on Elizabeth psychically, and I was able to channel some additional information. The room was as it had been before-cold, heavy, and sad. Elizabeth seemed very fearful, and would not manifest for us, but I could feel her very strongly. I felt the intensity of her labor pains; the hunger she had experienced from being starved; and the fear for her baby's safety as well as her own. My stomach cramped, my leg throbbed, and at one point, I was overcome with a choking sensation. With all the stress and abuse she suffered, it is amazing that this poor girl was able to deliver her baby at all. I spent some time trying to see if I could show her a way to the light, but Elizabeth's ghost is still too confused and grief-stricken to move on. Keep in mind, Ghosts do not experience time and distance as we do. For Elizabeth, her physical death seems like it was just yesterday.

After taking some photos, we walked back to find

the others. It was now almost 2:30 a.m., and we decided to pack everything up. The witching hour was just at hand, I didn't believe we would see anything else. As we stood around the front desk, preparing to leave, I verbally challenged George to show himself. I told him we were leaving, and I asked if he was too scared to manifest. After only a few seconds, we began to hear heavy footsteps above us. We waited, and nothing happened. For the next few minutes, he seemed to try and manipulate us by making noises when we would attempt to leave. Along with the heavy footsteps, we heard a clatter, and some banging in the basement. Groaning and other unearthly sounds echoed in our ears. George doesn't like the living to be in his hotel, but he hates to be challenged even more. I looked at the staircase, and there, on the first landing, I saw a brief glimpse of his shadow— not very solid. At the last minute, he changed his mind, and disappeared. This could have been because there were too many people around. Three times we started to leave, and every time he found a way to catch our attention. Tiring of his game, we realized he was not going to manifest, and we left the hotel.

Standing out front, I pointed to the second floor above the hotel sign, and told Shante and Maliena that George was there, watching us. I could see him psychically, with a cigar in his mouth and a smug look of victory. There was horrible, black, swirling energy all around him. We took several exterior photos, and then we left. When the film was developed, we caught a large, glowing orb in the exact spot I had pointed out, as well as another orb on the fourth floor. In the three pictures, the orb of George drifted from the balcony of the second floor, up to the third floor. (As I mentioned earlier, you can view photos of our trip on my website. The address is posted in Chapter One.)

Later, we listened to the audio tape-recorder that I had been carrying. It was filled with bleeps and glitches that should not have been there, and much of the text was nearly impossible to understand. No other tape we made on the trip came out like that. And even though the tape was sensitive enough to pick up the passing trucks outside, it did not record the wail or the moans.

CHANNELED INFORMATION

It was reveled to me that George Winfield was very attracted to my energy and followed me the whole time we were investigating. He was walking behind me, smelling my hair, and briefly touching me. My vibration, and my looks intrigued him. I am used to ghosts being attracted to my energy, but his attention was very sexual and disturbing. This ghost was not afraid of us, as so many are, and he was the one who pushed me on the stairs in the basement. In general, George is as evil and malevolent now as he was in life. He is about 5'11, a bit portly, with a big, bushy moustache and thin, slicked-back, dark hair. He dresses very nicely, in a suit with a long jacket, printed vest, and pocket-watch. George is always, smoking a cigar. He is a neurotic perfectionist, and I believe that he died from a heart attack. George thinks he is still running the hotel. He likes to stand by the elevator, and in the front of the second-story room, where he can look out onto the street. He still bullies Elizabeth, who is stuck in the hotel with him.

They both project images of the hotel being open, with the hustle and bustle of imaginary people. But as far as I can tell, they are the only two resident ghosts in the building. Other psychics have claimed to see a midget and two small children on the staircase. I did not see or feel their presence, but it could have something to do with the portal. Many spirits come and go through this portal, perhaps even darker entities.

The baby is not a ghost, as so many people have said, but is an energy imprint that continues to play out the tragedy. It was George who ordered the death of the newborn, but being a gutless coward, he had someone else do the dirty work for him.

Elizabeth is stuck, due to fear, grief and confusion: she feels just as trapped and enslaved as she did in life. Elizabeth was not a wealthy girl, and she was very young, maybe eighteen or nineteen years old. I didn't get a very good visual of Elizabeth's facial features, but I could see that she still wears only her nightgown. She was not a prostitute, as urban legend states. Her relationship with George was at one point sexual, but it is unclear if she was a mistress or an abused relative. On my second visit to Room 109, I started to get cramps and lower back pains, picking up on Elizabeth. During that walk-through, this is what I was able to channel. First of all, Elizabeth was very pregnant when she was chained to the radiator, maybe already as much as seven months. I couldn't believe that she didn't miscarry, due to the abuse she received. She was beaten, given very little food, not able to bathe or keep clean, and had a very badly injured right leg. Much of the time, she suffered from agonizing hunger pains, severe cramps, and back pains from the pregnancy. She also had many cuts and bruises, from George's beatings.

I saw Elizabeth carving something into the wall where the radiator was. However, the hotel is now so dilapidated, that it's impossible to tell what it was. If someone were to clean that wall, and apply some sort of specialized solution, there is a good chance that the message would come through. After she gave birth, George ordered one of his employees to throw the infant down the mineshaft. I saw this happen psychically, and I was appalled by how nonchalantly it all took place-like a meaningless chore the employee had been given.

At one point, George raped Elizabeth, but it was not clear if he was the baby's biological father. I believe Elizabeth died because George choked her to death.

The most astounding information I received, was the fact that this hotel was built atop a powerful vortex. This was the strongest vortex that I have ever encountered, much stronger than the famous one in Sedona, Arizona. Like suction in the building, the energy pulled and prodded us relentlessly, leaving a cold and tingly sensation on our skin. The land this hotel was built on is cursed, or so it would seem to many people. This location should never have been built upon, and no one should have attempted it. Because of the portal, no business will ever be able to survive. The vortex energy is most noticeable around the elevator, in the middle of the hotel, but most potent on the second floor. Whoever dug into the earth, creating the gold mines, opened a portal unleashing a vortex that rises high into the air, which can be strongly compared to the Bermuda Triangle. The energy is so intense, that it affects us physically. It's like a tear in the matrix was opened; it's definitely one of the few portals on earth that unlocks access to other dimensions. What does this mean? It means that this opening allows different creatures, ghosts, and entities to pass through; it is a doorway to other places. To walk into this hotel is to walk into two worlds at the same time. George and Elizabeth do not have to try and penetrate our reality, because the portal merges the two dimensions. Anyone approaching this portal will risk crossing through to another realm.

A description of another vortex, reported to exist in Puerto Rico, will provide you with a better understanding of what all this means. There's a documented case about this vortex, which has a portal that is similar to Goldfield's. It is also like a tear, or a crack in our world, leading to other worlds, and even to astral planes. On this island, ranchers began to complain of cattle mutilations. They would find their animals dead, with all the blood drained out of them. But, unlike with normal death, rigor mortis did not set in, as it should have. Then, the townspeople started reporting sightings of some sort of unearthly creature, flying through the night. It was a large, winged creature, with a face that almost looked human; it had red eyes and the body of an animal, like a gargoyle. The people began to call this creature Chupacabra, which means goat-sucker. This creature was sighted so often, that the Mayor of Puerto Rico even went on TV to talk about it. Finally, after several months, it was found dead, and its body displayed as proof that it had truly existed. This creature comes from a very low astral plane. It was never meant to be here on earth, but because of the portal, it found its way in.

The portal in the Goldfield Hotel is very similar. The energy it emits would allow a psychic medium to attract spirits to them, and you could even walk over into another realm. This energy forcibly raises your vibration, almost giving you the feeling of being high: it alters your state, and activates paranormal energy. My advice, to anyone who might be contemplating a visit to the Goldfield Hotel, is: "Don't go, it is much too dangerous!"

This hotel is not accessible to the public. If you should decide to seek permission and visit anyway, please use extreme caution, and be leery of what might emerge from that portal!

Ancient Egyptians believed that upon death they would be asked two questions and their answers would determine whether they could continue their journey in the afterlife.

The questions:

Did you bring joy? & Did you find joy?

– Leo Buscaglia

THE MONTE VISTA HOTEL
FLAGSTAFF, ARIZONA

HISTORY

*I*n 1881, Flagstaff began to grow with the new Atlantic and Pacific Railroad that pushed its way across America. By 1886, Flagstaff was the biggest city on the main railroad. The town was thriving with the logging industry, cow and sheep herding, and mining operations.

During the 1920's, Route 66 was built and passed right through town thus helping to make Flagstaff a popular tourist stop. The Monte Vista Hotel was built in 1926, at a cost of $200,000. It was a first-class, luxury hotel, built to support Flagstaff's rise in tourism. A twelve-year-old girl won a contest, to select the hotel's name. The Monte Vista's grand opening was January 1, 1927.

In 1931, when a major bootlegging operation was put to an end, the main speak-easy turned out to be the Monte Vista Hotel Lounge.

During the 1940's and 50's, when over 100 western films were shot around this area, the Monte Vista housed many celebrities. One room at The Monte Vista Hotel was in fact used for a scene in the movie Casablanca. The hotel belonged to the Flagstaff residents until the early 1960's, after which it was sold to a private individual. It was the longest, publicly owned commercial hotel in the history of America.

In the early 1990's, hotel owner Jim Craven restored the property to its original décor.

HAUNTED HISTORY

The Monte Vista Hotel is said to house several ghosts. Even John Wayne reported that he had seen a friendly ghost in his room (the same room in which we stayed, number 402).

Over the years, several hotel guests have described a "phantom bellboy," who likes to knock on doors, and speak in a muffled voice. But when the door is opened, no one is there.

In 1970, three men robbed a nearby bank, and one of them was shot. They ran into the Monte Vista to have some drinks. The wounded man died there, and his ghost is said to still haunt the hotel's lounge. Bartenders and patrons have witnessed barstools sliding around on their own, the feeling of a male presence in the back storage rooms, and the touch of ghostly hands on their shoulders, as they walk down the back hall.

In room 220, bed linens have been stripped when no one is there, and lights and televisions are said to turn on by themselves. Supposedly, this is all being caused by an eccentric, long-term boarder, who was in the habit of hanging raw meat from his hotel-room chandelier. He died in this room, and was not discovered until three days later.

During the early 1940's, two prostitutes were murdered in Room 306, and their bodies were flung from the window. Guests now say they feel the ghosts of these two murdered women, watching them.

Room 305 used to have a rocking chair, which would move to the window by itself. When guests left the room, the chair would be facing away from the window, and when they returned, it would be facing toward the window. A female apparition has been seen sitting in this chair at night.

Some people claim to have seen a dark shadow, roaming through the upstairs halls, and others have reported a sense of foreboding, or of being surrounded by negative energy.

Many reports about ghosts also revolve around the hair salon, which is connected to the building, a few doors down.

TRAVELOGUE

Day One: Monday, June 17, 11:30 p.m.

We drove for most of the day, stopping only to spend a few hours in Las Vegas. Finally very hot, and very tired, we arrived at the Monte Vista. After checking in, we took the old, shiny, metal elevator to room 402, also known as "The John Wayne Suite." Once we were inside the room we had a major complaint. No one told us in advance that there was no air-conditioning. This was a problem since the town was experiencing a heat wave. Our room on the fourth floor was unbearably hot upon arrival.

When the hotel was renovated, it was restored to its 1930's décor, and now it very much resembles its original appearance. Our suite was small, but charming. A small bathroom divided the two bedrooms, which were decorated with quaint bedspreads and lots of pillows. A spunky young man, working at the front desk, was nice enough to find us a window fan, which cooled things down considerably, and created a pleasant breeze. It was well past midnight when we finally settled in; we stayed up for awhile, but we were too tired to go exploring. Earlier, the front desk staff had told us we could have access to the entire hotel, any room that we wanted, provided it was not already occupied. But right then, we needed rest, more than anything else.

As soon as I tried going to sleep, I got a strong feeling that someone was watching me! A cold chill passed over my bed, and I began to feel a heavy vibration on my chest. After a few minutes, it started to really creep me out. Then I realized that two ghosts were watching us. The first ghost was that of a young woman, dressed in a nice outfit. I emphasize her clothes because they seemed to mean so much to her. She was wearing a long, lacey, skirt, with an impeccable, neatly tucked-in shirt, and seemed very fond of the white umbrella, which she was holding in her hand. She looked like some sort of a burlesque dancer. Her hair was pinned up, and the energy around her was very sensual, yet classy. I didn't feel that she possessed any negative feelings towards us, but I was not quite sure why she was watching us sleep. As I adjusted my eyes to the darkness of the room, and visualized her standing there, I felt a sense of sadness fall over her and the room. Maybe this poor woman simply missed being alive. There was also the dark shadow of a man. He seemed to be neither good nor bad, just a bit confused. After concentrating on him for a moment, I clarified that in life he had been crazy, and this discombobulated reality had carried over with him at his time of death. I couldn't make him out nearly as well as the woman. He stayed closer to the walls, and drifted back and forth, with his energy dispersing slightly. I got the impression that there was no contact at all between these two ghosts. Looking back on this incident, I realize it was a significant encounter, but at the time, I chalked it up as unnerving, at best.

Day Two: Tuesday, June 18, 5:30 p.m.

We got the keys to the rooms that were supposed to be haunted, but when we went through them, the only one that seemed to carry any paranormal energy was room 305. Here, I felt the woman's presence from the previous night, only more strongly. It was definitely the room she was murdered in. I got the feeling that this woman was a ghostly observer; she had no desire to interact with anyone, living or dead, but was content to wander around the hotel. This room was definitely home base for her. She is the ghost responsible for the moving chair, and she really does like to sit and look out the window. In some of the other rooms, there was residual energy, and a few cold spots, but not enough to try and stake out.

We decided to keep the key to room 305, and return for surveillance later that night. We placed one chair in a certain position (although there was no rocking chair to be found), and we left.

About an hour later, while in the lounge, I was approached by a woman who had taken a picture earlier in the day, and wanted me to verify if what she had captured was a spirit, or just a light flare in her film. It was definitely a spirit, floating perfectly in the background of the photo. The spirit was so visible, that it caught the attention of the night desk clerk. He was quite a skeptical fellow, but possessed a whimsical sense of humor that we all enjoyed, and even though most of his comments dripped with sarcasm, not even he could scoff at the ghost captured in the picture. The next morning, the woman who had showed us the photograph was kind enough to give us a copy she had made.

June 18, 11:30 p.m.

The three of us ventured back down to room 305. Everything was quiet: the chair had not noticeably moved, and the energy didn't feel particularly heavy. I spent about half-an-hour channeling information and feeling the place out; after setting up the camera we left. Awhile later, Maliena went back to the lounge and spoke to a few of the hotel's employees. (One worked at the adjoining hair salon that is also reportedly haunted.) They mentioned that the hall connecting to the lounge was known to have a lot of paranormal activity around midnight. Maliena went to explore, but she didn't see anything. She felt the usual heaviness, and a sense that someone was watching her, but not with the same intensity, that many others had claimed to feel.

One of the hotel's security guards said that he often felt like someone was sneaking up behind him, as he walked down the hall after shutting off the lights. He also claimed to have felt, on more than one occasion, the ominous weight of unidentifiable hands, grabbing on to his shoulders. A front-desk clerk reported that she had seen chairs in the lobby, moving on their own.

Jason, an employee of the hair salon, related another event. Apparently, the salon had once been the post office, and now is a split-level store. Jason said he is still skeptical, and somewhat uncertain, about "exactly what" he experienced one night, when he was closing up the shop alone. He had gone upstairs to grab his keys, and when he turned around he was hit by an icy, cold chill. Suddenly, he smelled something indescribably horrid and foul; he said that it felt like pure evil, and seemed very malevolent. Freaked out, he ran downstairs as fast as he could, locked up, and left.

A few months later, when Jason stayed at the Monte Vista in room 214, he had another experience. In the middle of the night, he woke up feeling disoriented. He looked around, and realized that he could see his own breath. When he glanced at the wall, he saw shadows, dancing about. He said he refused to acknowledge them, and squeezed his eyes shut until they disappeared.

After Maliena returned to the room, we decided to walk through the building, one last time, before turning in for the night. We did not capture anything on film, and aside from a group of kids doing some late-night research; we didn't run into anything out of the ordinary. We left the hotel, the next morning. Our basic conclusion was that the Monte Vista Hotel is definitely haunted, but the haunting are not as active as urban legend suggests.

CHANNELED INFORMATION

I picked up on two prominent ghosts at the Monte Vista, and was able to verify two of the stories. First, the man from room 220 is as crazy in death as he was in life! This man only shows himself in the form of a dark shadow. He likes to roam the halls, and enter the guestrooms. He also is very fond of the elevator, which is original to the building. Sometimes he "plays" with hotel guests who are inside, by stopping the elevator between floors or not allowing the elevator to move at all. Guests are left waiting for the elevator for long periods of time, until eventually they just give up and take the stairs.

Shante and Maliena experienced this, while attempting to head down to the lobby. The doors seemed unable to make up their mind as to whether or not they would close. This made the girls feel uneasy, and they got off and took the stairs. This ghost is harmless enough, but it is a bit disconcerting, to feel him watching you when you are in the shower or in bed. It is especially unnerving when you get on the elevator, and realize halfway down that you are not alone!

Most of the channeled information I received related to the woman in room 305. Rumors say she was a prostitute, who had been murdered. This female ghost appeared to me wearing a lacey, long skirt that looked like a costume; she showed herself with her hair done up in curls. She was an entertainer of some sort, possibly a burlesque dancer. This lady, also a high-class prostitute, was more refined than most of the other "working girls" in town, and more particular about her clientele. She had a lot of style and grace, and always presented herself to the public as "a lady." She considered herself a step above her roommate, Cathleen, a dark-haired, less- desirable prostitute. Both of these women were murdered at the same time. The "lady" in room 305 frequently entertained a particular man, who lost his temper with her one day, while in a drunken rage. It was like "a deal gone bad." Within minutes, the argument heated to a point of no return, and the man attacked both women with a knife. Although Cathleen was not involved in the argument, she was a victim of circumstance, and she too was slain. Both women were beaten, stabbed, and thrown from the window, face first. But one didn't die until she hit her head and broke her neck. Technically, it was the fall that killed her, and not the stabbing. As attention was drawn to the women lying on the street, the man hurried down the stairs and out of the building. He was never caught.

The female ghost likes to move the rocking chair to the window, so she can look outside. In life, she loved to gaze out of the window, and that is what she would do to attract people's attention. The "working girls" used to spend a lot of time in their rooms, and the large, open windows provided a convenient way for them to communicate with the people on the street. This woman is also the one who was watching us, the first night in our room. She wanders from room to room, much like the male ghost, but she prefers room 305.

Death...The last sleep?

No, it is the final awakening.

– Walter Scott

TOMBSTONE
TOMBSTONE, ARIZONA

TOWN HISTORY

*I*n the late 1800's, when Tombstone was at its boom, Allen Street was the center of town. Only half-a-mile long, the street was home to over 150 saloons, most of them also brothels. The streets of Tombstone contain a lot of history, and many events that happened there were as fascinating as they were horrifying. While the area became notorious for saloons, gambling halls and the shootout at the O.K. Corral, Tombstone was also recognized as the most sophisticated city in the West.

Tombstone's Birdcage Theater was one of its most renowned establishments. Built in the 1880's, the Birdcage was an entertainment theater, a gambling house, a saloon, and a "house of ill repute." Many well-known performers appeared on the theater's stage, including Josephine Sarah Marcus, who became Wyatt Earp's girlfriend, Eddy Foy, and Lily Langtree. In 1882,

The New York Times described the Birdcage as "the wildest and wickedest nightspot in the West." The Birdcage kept its doors open, twenty-four hours a day for nine years, never closing once, despite some sixteen odd gun and knife fights, which killed over twenty-six people and left around 140 bullet holes, sporadically spaced, throughout its walls and ceilings.

In addition to the "good ol' gunfights," some rather unbelievable acts of violence also occurred at the Birdcage. Especially shocking is the story of Margarita, who worked at the Birdcage as an entertainer. According to legend, one evening Margarita was sitting on the lap of Billy Milgreen, a well-known gambler. "Gold-dollar," Billy's girlfriend, discovered Margarita moving in on her man, and, in a fit of rage, pulled out a double-edged stiletto, attacked Margarita, and literally cut her heart out. Covered in blood, Gold-dollar ran out the back door of the theater. She was never brought up on charges, because no one could ever find the weapon. Over 100 years later, the stiletto was found buried behind the theater, and it is now on display inside.

The Birdcage served a variety of purposes, including use as a massive gambling hall. The high-stakes table was hidden in a private area beneath the stage. It was complete with its own bar, and in close proximity to the prostitutes' sleeping quarters. Two of its more famous patrons were Doc Holiday and Wyatt Earp. Bets started at a minimum of $1,000, and during one eight-year span, gambling worth more than $10,000,000 took place. Wealthy gamblers often came to town and waited days before a seat would open up at the legendary high stakes table.

HAUNTED HISTORY

Tombstone was not included on our original itinerary. However, we found so much research about the town's haunted buildings, we decided it might be beneficial to take a slight detour there, especially since it was on the way to our next destination. There was information about ghostly cowboys, who had hung out at "Big Nose Kate's Saloon," and about the ghost of a woman known to wander around the Birdcage Theater. This woman was reported to have stopped traffic, on several different occasions, by walking into the middle of the street and then disappearing. There were also numerous accounts, by those who had seen them, of the ghosts of a woman and a man who frequented the Birdcage Theater's balcony.

When we heard about the ghosts reportedly still haunting this Wild West town, our curiosity was definitely aroused. We decided to stop there, not because we expected anything to happen, but to satisfy our insatiable desire to investigate, for ourselves, the research we had found.

TRAVELOGUE

Wednesday, June 19, afternoon

Our "slight detour" took longer than anticipated. We had to leave the main highway, Interstate 10, and drive nearly half-an-hour, around twenty-three miles down a lonely, old, two-lane road, until we finally arrived at the top of a bluff, also called Tombstone. In the end, our decision to visit the town proved worthy of the effort.

Tombstone has preserved its "heart of the Old West atmosphere," and Allen Street still hosts an assortment of beautifully restored, fully functioning saloons. It's an amazing sight: old-timers sit out on the porches of the town's wooden buildings, smoking their pipes, and gazing at the rugged, dust-devil-filled terrain. Modern day cowboys stroll the boardwalks with spurs jingling getting ready for the next reenactment at the OK corral.

The Birdcage Theater, Tombstone's most infamous building, offers an amazing tour. It's easy to understand why so many people believe that its haunted. The theater was closed for over fifty years, literally boarded-up, and left "as is": tabletops covered with bottles; chairs flipped upside down; card games left half-finished. When a decision was made to reopen the Birdcage as a museum/gift-shop, Plexiglas was used to surround its delicate furnishings, and ropes were used to separate other areas that might be harmed. The Birdcage looks exactly like it did during its heyday in the Old West, the upper level box seats were constructed as small rooms that over look the entire theater, usually the gentlemen would be accompanied by a well dressed woman or sometimes two, hence the balcony rooms where called "bird cages". These rooms are still complete with cane chairs, gold gilt framed pictures, and velvet drapes that could be drawn for privacy. Below on the main level was the stage with its original hand-painted backdrop. An old, upright piano still sits there along side. A sign hangs on the wall telling the prostitutes where to turn in their tips and how much of a percentage to give the house. Everything is on display, including many of the prostitute's licenses. Back then, prostitution was a legal trade, the sheriff signed the licenses. Today they are framed, and when possible, accompanied by each woman's photograph, placed beside them. It is a fascinating display. Even the bullet holes in the walls and ceilings are still visible, indicating where many long-dead cowboys shot off their pistols. Also on view is one of the original, horse-drawn, glass sided funeral carriages, in fairly good condition.

The entire street has been kept as authentic as possible. There are wood plank sidewalks, horse-drawn carriage tours, and bars with their original saloon names, whose walls are hung with guns, trinkets and forgotten letters, written by the town's actual residents.

We visited one of Tombstone's cemeteries and walked around the old graves, some marked only with sticks, bound together to form a cross. Most of the names were eroded from the gravestones by the dust that blew over them year after year. Iron fences outlined small family plots and crypts. Some of the plots were decorated with dying flowers, while others probably hadn't been visited by a living relative in decades. Being in Tombstone was literally "a trip back in time." You felt like you had truly returned to this era, and could better understand the hardships these people once endured. This town is a wonderful side trip for anyone who wants to experience the authentic old west.

CHANNELED INFORMATION

Because this book is dedicated to ghosts, I decided that each chapter should contain at least some sort of ghost story. I really enjoyed Tombstone, and I feel that this ghost town deserves recognition. In order to remain true to the book's intention, I went into prayer for a long time, and was able to channel some of Tombstone's wayward spirits.

The first bit of information I received concerns the woman at the Birdcage Theater. Her ghost is seen throughout the building, but on several occasions was reported to be in the street, during the middle of the day. Some even said she stopped traffic, before disappearing from view.

This woman is the ghost of a prostitute, from the late 1880's. She was crossing the street in the middle of the day, and a horse-drawn carriage ran over her, crushing her body and killing her. This death was tragic and untimely. The girl was young, and had a hard life. As a result, she chooses to stay as a ghost, seeing Tombstone the way it used to be, and sometimes interacting with the living people.

Outside on Allen Street, two older gunslingers are a couple of other prominent ghosts. They were friends in life, and died together in the street outside the Birdcage. My spirit guides told me that they frequent many of the bars, but prefer the Birdcage. Many times people have heard them walking up and down Tombstone's wooden walkways, with the spurs from their boots clanking noisily.

The Birdcage Theater is host to five resident ghosts. The prostitute mentioned earlier, the two gunslingers, and an aristocratic, married couple, also from the late 1880's. They show themselves in the balcony of the theater, dressed in evening attire. The woman's hair is pinned up, she wears an elegant, emerald-green satin dress, and she is adorned with jewels. Although this couple's names were not provided, it was clear that they were well-liked residents of the town, probably important business owners of some sort. They had been at the Birdcage one evening to watch a show, when a gunfight broke out. They were accidentally shot and killed when they got caught in crossfire.

These ghosts all seem to have one thing in common: they don't usually interact with the living people. They prefer to manifest their own surroundings. The way they remember things to be. To them, Tombstone is still very much the "Wild, Wild, West." Creating the way Tombstone looked when they were alive is even easier for them to project, since the buildings have stayed so much the same, and most of today's residents make their living by keeping the old traditions alive!

The day which we fear as our last

is but the birthday of eternity.

— Seneca

THE LODGE
CLOUDCROFT, NEW MEXICO

TOWN HISTORY

*T*he town of Cloudcroft was proposed, purchased and filed by the railroad, in June of 1899. The original translation of "Cloudcroft" was "Pasture in the Clouds." The Lodge, in Cloudcroft is located deep in New Mexico's Sacramento Mountains, and was built by the railroad in 1901, to attract tourists. Originally, the Lodge consisted of forty tents, set up on platforms, for people to sleep in, an entertainment area, a dining room, a kitchen, and a parlor.

The Lodge burned down in 1909, and was rebuilt in 1911. In 1924, the railroad sold the Lodge to a private owner. In 1936, Mr. Carr, of the Southwest Lumber Company, purchased the Lodge, which he sold during the Second World War. By 1938, America's railroad travel was beginning to decline. As a result, train service to Cloudcroft ended in 1947, less than ten years later.

Over the years, The Cloudcroft Lodge, located in the

middle of a magnificent forest, has become a cozy and beautiful establishment. Its various amenities include a golf course, a pool with Jacuzzi and sauna, and a fabulous, five-star restaurant.

HAUNTED HISTORY

Due to all the changes that occurred during the town's growth, including the destruction, renovation, and multiple ownership of The Lodge, it's understandable why there are no official details about the murder of Rebecca, a hotel chambermaid during the early 1930's. No documented facts exist, only rumors and speculation. Most of the hotel's rooms contain some sort of memoir of "Rebecca," including the popular "Rebecca's Restaurant," but beside the fact that she was a beautiful redhead who worked at The Lodge and loved it there, no one seems to know very much about her. After Rebecca disappeared, people feared that her lumberjack boyfriend probably murdered her, when he caught her with another man. But neither Rebecca's body nor any evidence of a crime was ever found. So, the lumberjack went free, and the ghost of Rebecca was left to wander the vast estate, alone.

Rebecca reportedly haunts the following areas: "The Governor's Suite" (she is said to be partial to a particular telephone there); the Red-Dog Saloon; and the tower—where apparitions of her have been documented.

A guest once claimed to have seen Rebecca's ghost soaking in his bathtub. When he reported this to the front desk, the clerks came to investigate, but she was gone.

The night desk clerk told us another interesting tale about Rebecca. One evening, as he was setting up the dining room for breakfast, he suddenly noticed a glowing, white point of light, dancing around the ceiling. It lasted for a few seconds, then disappeared. He thought it might be Rebecca, but more likely just the ceiling light, playing tricks on him; so, he went about his business. Awhile later, a man phoned down to say that he had just been awakened "by some sort of a light," which bounced around his room and then vanished through the floor. This guest's room was directly above the dining room, and the incident happened almost simultaneously with what happened to the night desk clerk.

TRAVELOGUE

Day One: Wednesday, June 19, 9:30 p.m.

Except for our side-trip to Tombstone, we spent the rest of this day "on the road." It seemed like an eternity, before we finally reached the city of Alamogordo, New

Mexico. From there, it was another thirty-minute drive, up a steep incline (4,000 feet above sea level), to Cloudcroft.

We checked in to the Lodge, and the front desk clerk took us on a short tour. He then told us we were welcome to roam about as we pleased.

The lodge was gorgeous, and our "Governor's Suite" exceeded all expectations: double doors led to a small, quaint parlor, with its own little chandelier; there was a foyer, a living room, a bedroom, and a bathroom, all charmingly decorated in a Victorian theme. After we unpacked and settled in, Maliena and I decided to look around. Starting at our door, we worked our way down the hall, up to the second floor (which led to the Honeymoon Suite), then back down past two small gift-shops, and into the lobby. We passed the bar area, which was closing up because it was so late. The night desk clerk was setting up the dining area, and he talked to us about his personal encounter with Rebecca. The entire lodge was filled with paintings of Rebecca, and we noticed that her picture had even been reproduced in a large, stained-glass window. She was very beautiful, with long, fire-red, curly hair, and striking green eyes. Because so much of the Lodge is dedicated to her image, it is no wonder Rebecca likes it there. Her face was even engraved on the backs of the wooden oak chairs in our room.

We went outside to explore the back of the property, and found the deck, with a swimming pool and sauna, and the golf course, off in the distance. We finished the night by checking out the old chambermaids' quarters, where I felt a lot of paranormal energy but didn't see anything. As I walked softly down the cramped hallway, I felt Rebecca's energy-faint, but present—all around us. She is a very sexual and flirtatious ghost. We tried to get into the tower, but it was locked, and we didn't think we would be able to obtain a key so late at night. The hallway leading to the back tower door was filled with moths, which mostly lay dormant on the ceiling; but one wrong move sent scores of them swooshing past our heads. It was kind of spooky, how all the halls and doors led to each other and how quiet everything was.

About an hour later, we returned to our room. I tried to fall asleep, but was kept awake by strange tapping and scratching noises, which seemed to be coming from the walls. At first, I thought there was an animal outside, but it didn't quite sound like one. Maliena also heard it from her room, but neither of us was ever able to identify it. Aside from these sounds, nothing else bothered us, and we finally managed to get some much-needed rest.

Day Two: Thursday, June 20, 12 p.m.

The day was rainy and quiet, and I spent a lot of time alone. Maliena spent most of the day decoding tape recordings and notes. Shante was also busy, reflecting on the notes she had taken. But I felt a compulsion to comb the grounds, one more time. I was casually browsing in one of the gift-shops, when I felt a sudden, sharp tug on the back of my cloak. (I assumed it was Rebecca.) I turned immediately, but no one was there—just a cold spot. I took that gesture as a playful "hello" from Rebecca, and went about my business, glancing around periodically, in spite of myself. I looked at the salesclerk behind the counter, but she was unaware that anything had just happened.

I returned to the lobby, to sit on one of the comfortable leather couches. During our entire stay, The Lodge was quite deserted, so I had ample opportunity to meditate undisturbed, and channel information from Rebecca's ghost.

I was able to tap directly into Rebecca's energy, and channel an enormous amount of information, which allowed me to solve some very old mysteries.

Later that afternoon, we finally made it up to the tower, which we felt was a bit scary. I knew instantly that Rebecca was very fond of this area; she still spends a lot of time here, but she also travels in the astral realms, so she isn't always around. We gazed out of the tower lookout, and noticed a good-sized windstorm brewing. The eerie stillness of the mountain was overwhelming. We stayed in the tower for about half an hour, but Rebecca did not appear. We returned to our room, and headed down for dinner.

After a leisurely, excellent meal, Maliena left, hoping to take a sauna. But the rain, the cold, and the wind prevented the sauna from heating up, so she quickly returned. I decided to relay what I had learned from my channeling session, and we wrote everything down. Unfortunately, this night proved to be as uneventful as the previous one had been. Despite the hours we spent looking around, Rebecca would not manifest for me. However, there is still a great deal of information to report, thanks to the channeled information I received, and the many amazing stories we heard.

Just the experience of staying at the Lodge was wonderful, in itself. The mountains were breathtaking, and on our way up, I saw my very first elk!

CHANNELED INFORMATION

The main mystery I was able to solve about Rebecca was why no one ever pursued her disappearance. I learned that Rebecca emigrated from Ireland to the United States in the early 1930's, and got a job as a chambermaid. She made a few friends, but had no relatives here, and when she disappeared, no one knew anything about her, or whom to notify. She was a young girl, isolated in the mountains of New Mexico, and an easy target for a horrible crime.

The first thing that came to me was that Rebecca doesn't just haunt a few areas of the Lodge. True, her essence is very strong there, but Rebecca is a curious, flirtatious, nosey ghost. She loves all of the grounds around the hotel, especially the golf course, because she enjoys all the men. Psychically, Rebecca showed me how she likes to wander the golf course, flirting with the men and playing practical jokes on them, which most of the time they don't realize she is doing.

Rebecca did not have a strong, religious background, and at the time of her death, she went to a astral level, which she believed was as far as she could go. As a result, she spends her time there, and at the Lodge. She really thinks that this is what happens to everyone when they die, and that this is where she is supposed to be.

Along with her love for the Lodge, Rebecca also loved men, and at one point she had a boyfriend who was a lumberjack. He was a big, burly man, with dark hair and a red-tinged beard. He was a heavy drinker, who became mean and nasty when he was drunk. He tried to control Rebecca, was overly possessive, and felt that he "owned" her. But Rebecca did not feel "owned" by him, or anyone else. Because of his work, the lumberjack was often away from the Lodge for weeks or months at a time, and eventually Rebecca met another man and fell in love.

The lumberjack, who still believed Rebecca belonged to him, came to the Lodge one night and found her with the other man. Although there was no solid proof, the implication was there, and the lumberjack knew in his heart that Rebecca loved another. Enraged, he left. But he returned just before dawn, and forced Rebecca to leave with him. Very frightened, and still in her nightgown, she reluctantly went with him. She thought that she could sweet-talk her way out of it, and bring him to his senses, but it didn't work. The lumberjack dragged her deeper and deeper into the woods, where they began to argue and fight. Rebecca showed me images of a serious head trauma, which happened when the jealous lumberjack pushed her, and she hit her head on the ground, splitting it open. This didn't kill her, but stunned her enough to disorient her. It was probably a merciful injury, because at that point the lumberjack lifted his axe and chopped her to pieces. I'm not quite clear about what he did with her body, but from what I saw psychically, whatever wasn't buried, the animals got to. The people at the Lodge suspected that he killed her, but with no physical body, and no other evidence, there was nothing they could do. Since Rebecca was an immigrant, and had no family here, no one pursued the matter.

Rebecca knew she had been killed, but was confused about what happens at the time of death. She really believes that she belongs here, and she has been roaming the grounds of the Lodge, and the astral level, ever since—blissfully ignorant to the call of her angels and guides, who wish to help her cross over to the other side.

On the morning of our departure, Ed Thomas, the night desk clerk, had left us an envelope, which included some additional facts about the Lodge, and a report about another personal encounter. This encounter had not been with Rebecca, but with some "other" force! He told us we could tell his tale, and we copied it word for word, so as not to distort any facts. It is certainly an illustration of the supernatural energy that seems to emanate from the Cloudcroft Lodge.

THE UNRULY GUEST ON FRIDAY THE 13th
By Ed Thomas

"I work as the night auditor at the Lodge in

Cloudcroft, New Mexico. The Lodge is a one- hundred-year-old resort hotel, with charming Bavarian architecture. It is located high on top of a mountain, at 9200 feet elevation. The immediate environment is that of a deep forest of fir, spruce, and pine. The Lodge sits above most of the trees, and the view to the West, looking down to the Tularosa Basin and the White Sands National Monument, is truly spectacular.

The main entrance to the Lodge is on its west side. As one enters the hallway, the front desk is on the left. Just past the front desk, the hallway opens to a large lobby, complete with nice chairs and couches and a huge fireplace. On the east side of the lobby are double doors leading out to the lawn, swimming pool, sauna, and hot tub. The distance from the west doors to the east doors is approximately thirty-five to forty yards.

I work from 10:00 p.m. until 8:00 a.m. My workstation is behind the front desk. From there, I can see anyone entering from the West because they have to pass right in front of me. I can look to my left and see the double doors on the east side of the lobby. Since I am an "outdoorsy" type of person, and since it usually gets pretty warm where I am working because of the heat from the lights and lack of air circulation in that area, I normally leave both sets of doors open for my entire shift.

My main duty is that of doing the nightly audit, but since I am the only one working during those hours, I have to take care of whatever else comes along. Most of the time "whatever else comes along" consists of a few late arrivals, or some early checkouts, a few phone calls, and maybe a reservation or two. Still, since I am the only one working, I have to take care of "whatever else comes along."

The situation I am going to tell you about happened on a beautiful August morning. The weather was clear, and it was 62 degrees. The sky was full of twinkling stars. They looked so close you could reach out and touch them. In other words, a typical August, Cloudcroft morning. The only thing different was the fact that this was Friday the thirteenth!

I was up to my eyebrows in paperwork. Suddenly, I was jolted out of my pencil-pushing endeavors by a loud Thump, and what sounded like bottles bumping together or dishes clashing together. I looked at my watch. It was 3:41 a.m. My first thought was "that must be Rebecca." Rebecca is our resident ghost. There was that noise again! Actually, it was a continuation of the noise. Thump, Clatter, Clatter, Clatter! This falls into the category I mentioned earlier, of "whatever else comes along." I decided I had better go see what was making the noise. It sounded like it had come from outside, so I went out to look. Outside, everything looked undisturbed. I started back inside. Then I heard it again! This time it was a muffled sound and it was coming from the area of the lounge and dining room. I went into the lounge and there he was! It was not Rebecca or any other ghost. He was real and he was alive! He must have been wearing his sneakers because I sure didn't see him or hear him come in, but there he was, big as life! I was standing there, looking eyeball to eyeball into the face of the wildest, meanest, roughest-looking character I had seen in awhile. His hair looked like he hadn't combed it or brushed it for quite some time, and he smelled like he hadn't had a bath in just as long a time.

I said, "Good morning, Sir. The lounge and the dining room are both closed. Could I help you with something?" He didn't say a word. He just stood there and stared at me and grunted a little. Then I saw it. He had torn up one of the nice leather chairs in the dining room and he had pulled a tablecloth and all the dishes off one of the tables. I said, "Sir, I don't know what the problem is, but I am sure we can get it worked out. Would you step out to the lobby with me?" He still didn't answer me, but he followed me out into the lobby. I didn't know what kind of situation I had gotten into. Why had he done the damage in the dining room? What else was he going to do? Was he going to turn on me?

Before I could finish my thoughts, he had started upstairs. "Sir, you can't go up there unless you're a guest of the Lodge! Our guests are asleep. Don't wake them up!" He continued up the stairs. I decided it might be best to let him have a look at the upstairs hall, rather than get into a confrontation with him up there and cause a commotion that might disturb the guests. I gave him four or five minutes and he didn't return, so I felt that I should try to roust him out. I started around the corner from the hallway in the lobby and up the stairs, and met him at the bottom of the stairs. I guess I startled him just about as much as he startled me. He turned quickly and ran downstairs. "Sir, there is nothing down there except offices and work areas. If you will just talk to me I am sure someone from management will be happy to work with you during regular business hours." He didn't say a word. It was like he didn't understand a word I was saying to him.

I still didn't know what was going on. Had he been drinking? Was he on drugs? Was he upset with someone here at the Lodge? Was he just plain crazy? At that point, I felt it was best to get some professional assistance. I called the Cloudcroft Police Department. Police Chief Gene Green was here almost immediately. I told the Chief what I had experienced and that he was still downstairs. Together we went downstairs.

In the hallway downstairs, we found trash scattered around. We continued down the hall. The trash container by the copy machine had been picked up, dumped completely, and the trash scattered all over the place. The trash container in the sales office had met the same fate. In the sales office, he had also knocked a computer and telephone off a desk and turned a chair over.

I looked to my left and saw that the door to the Reservations Office was closed. I said, "At least he didn't get in there." But where was he? I thought maybe he had gone into the laundry to sleep it off. I started to look for him. Suddenly, Chief Green said, "He's off in the Reservations Office. We could see by looking through the small window in the door that he was in there. I don't know what the ladies in reservations had done to him to upset him so much but it was quite obvious that he was very upset. He had knocked a computer, telephone, calculator, and everything else off one of the desks. He had then turned the desk upside down and he had dumped and scattered all the files from the desk and all of the trash in that office. "Don't worry about trying to take him into custody in here, Chief. Let's just get him outside before he does any more damage!"

Back down the hall, a short distance by the copy machine, there is a small hallway leading to an outside door. "I'll open this side door so we can get him outside and then deal with him out there!" After opening the door, I positioned myself just north of the side hall, determined that he was not going to get past me. Chief Green opened the door to the Reservations Office. "Come out of there with your paw in the air!" Nothing. We waited a minute or two, and still nothing. "Come out of there!" the Chief yelled. He started easing his way out the door. "Get on out of here!" At that, he started running toward me. I waited until he got almost to me. Then I jumped at him and yelled, "Get out of here! Go on out that door!"

For the first time since I met him (some forty-five minutes now), he seemed to understand what I was saying to him. He still didn't say anything. He just grunted a little and ran out the door like a Wild Man.... uh...er.... Wild Bear that is. Yes, he was a black bear about two years old and weighing about 175 to 185 pounds.

He ran across the lawn and jumped into the pond in front of the Lodge. He stayed in the pond for a few minutes (no doubt taking his much-needed bath) and then strolled off into the woods.

Of course, there was much discussion and speculation around the Lodge about the situation later in the day. Out of the entire discussion and speculation, one conclusion was reached. It was decided that the reason he finally listened to me, is because I look so much like Grizzly Adams, the bear thought I was Grizzly Adams!"

And so concludes Ed Thomas' account of that strange encounter. So how could a man transform into a bear, or did the bear transform into a man? I guess seeing is believing, as is true with most things. And regardless of speculation, Ed Thomas really did see more than he wanted to!

CHANNELED INFORMATION

I went into prayer and asked my spirit guides about this story. They told me that indeed it was a bear from the woods, which had the ability to change into a man for a brief time, and then back into a bear. The bear was very hungry and agitated, and felt almost dazed. From its form as a bear, it shifted into a form as a man, to search for food in a more lucrative location.

For what it is to die,

but to stand in the sun and melt into the wind?

And when the earth has claimed our limbs, then

we shall truly dance.

– Kahil Gibran

THE MYRTLES
SAINT FRANCISVILLE, LOUISIANA

PLANTATION HISTORY

*G*eneral David Bradford built what is now called "The Myrtles Plantation", in 1796. The General was an officer in George Washington's army, who was involved with "The Whiskey Rebellion." Despite the fact that he wasn't one of the sixteen men who organized the rebellion, he was branded as a traitor, and a warrant was issued for his arrest. He avoided a trial, and inevitable hanging, by escaping the troops and fleeing to Louisiana.

At this time, Louisiana was under Spanish control. It was considered foreign soil, so General Bradford was safe. He bought 650 acres of land from the Spanish government, at $1.25 per acre, and built a new home, which he named "The Laurel Grove Plantation." At this time, indigo was the plantation's main, cash-producing crop. The first house had only eight rooms, about half the number it has now, and the kitchen was a separate building built behind the pond. When this kitchen burned down, a second kitchen was built near the main house.

Eventually, Governor Bradford's name was cleared, and the government of Pennsylvania, his home state, granted him a pardon in 1800. But General Bradford decided not to return to Pennsylvania to live. Instead, he moved his family and belongings to the plantation he had built in Louisiana, and thirteen people had to squeeze into a small eight-room house.

Bradford's youngest daughter, Matilda, almost 15, was the last child at home. In 1815, the General betrothed her to his law partner, Judge Clark Woodruff, because he was afraid that she might become an old maid. They married when Matilda was seventeen and the Judge was forty.

When General Bradford died of yellow fever, he left the plantation to the Woodruffs, who moved in shortly thereafter. Matilda and the Judge were on their honeymoon to the West Indies, when she discovered the sweet smelling Crepe Myrtle tree. Matilda so admired these trees, that the Judge imported 150 of them as a special gift for her, and had them planted around the plantation. In 1819, the Woodruffs renamed their home "The Myrtles," and it has kept this name ever since.

The Woodruffs' first order of business was to change the plantation's main crop from indigo to cotton.

When greater income was generated from the cotton crop, the Woodruffs could afford to build additions to their house. These additions were completed in 1831.

Around 1827, after his second child was born, Judge Woodruff became attracted to a slave girl named Chloe. She became his mistress, and he brought her into the main house to look after the children. She remained there for almost seven years.

By 1834, The Woodruffs had three children, aged thirteen, seven, and five. The two youngest were born two years and two days apart, so the family celebrated their birthdays together.

After awhile, Chloe became overconfident with her prestigious household position, and started eavesdropping on family discussions. She was caught and reprimanded, although this was a serious offense. The third time this happened, the Judge vowed that she would learn her lesson. Chloe had been eavesdropping on a business deal, when the Judge discovered her kneeling against the Gentlemen's Parlor door, with her ear pressed up against it, the Judge decided that Chloe should be banished to the kitchen, which was separate from the main house. As additional punishment, he ordered that her left ear be cut off. From that day forward, Chloe wore a turban to hide the missing ear.

Several months later, Chloe realized she wasn't

going to be allowed to return to her job at the main house. She thought if she could prove to the family that they needed her, it would be her ticket back into their good graces. So she devised a plan. The two children were getting ready to celebrate their joint birthday, and Chloe convinced the head cook to allow her to bake a special cake. She had decided to boil the poisonous oleander plant into a liquid similar to arsenic. She knew that if she added a small dose to the cake, it would make the family sick. She thought everyone would panic, if they were sickened by something whose origin was unknown. Because no doctor would be able to get there in time, or diagnose what was wrong, they would call upon Chloe, who was knowledgeable about illness and herbal remedies. Chloe was confident that she would cure the family, and they would view her as their savior. General Bradford would then be so grateful, that he would reinstate her to her previous position.

Unfortunately, the slave did not understand the plant as well as she thought. She used too much poison, and it killed Matilda and the two youngest children. After the funerals, Judge Woodruff moved to New Orleans with his surviving daughter Octavia. He sold the plantation in 1836, and sent a list of household servants he wanted brought to his new home. Chloe's name was not on the list, and the prospect of remaining at The

Myrtles for the rest of her life was more than she could bear. Overcome with guilt and pain, she admitted to the other slaves what she had done.

Out of respect for the Woodruffs, the slaves caught Chloé, hanged her, and threw her body into the Mississippi River. Many of the slaves practiced voodoo and Santeria, and believed that a spirit could come back for you, if you carried the stench of death on your hands. For this reason, it is more likely that Chloe was hanged by the river, and not at the plantation.

In 1836, Rutherford Sterling purchased The Myrtles, and 2000 acres, for $2.75 an acre. He then began extensive remodeling, which led to the grandeur you see today. The improvements include elaborate ironwork, and a huge chandelier in the front foyer, which was hung in 1845. Mrs. Sterling bought the chandelier in France, for $1.50. It is made of crystal and iron, and weighs over 350 pounds. Some of the chandelier's crystals weigh as much as three pounds each.

HAUNTED HISTORY

Reportedly, The Myrtles is haunted by Chloe's ghost. Her image has even been photographed, appearing on many pictures in great detail.

The two children she poisoned are also supposedly

on the grounds. Mysterious child-sized handprints have been discovered, high up on windows, in places impossible to reach, and many claim to have heard the children laughing. There have been reports of guests being awakened by children jumping on their beds, especially in the "William Winters Suite." In one photograph, the children's images appeared in the treetops, as shadows with very clear outlines.

Some people claim to have heard General Bradford coughing in his bedroom, as he did when he was sick with yellow fever.

There have been reports of a groundskeeper, occasionally standing at the front gate. This ghost tells potential guests that the plantation is closed.

Once, a woman was trying to photograph her children, as they played on the back lawn's bridge. When the picture was developed, it showed wispy images of soldiers, wearing red coats, knickers and white stockings. They were covered in bandages and holding guns, as if marching across the lawn. Their uniforms suggest that they were from the Spanish-American war of 1886.

Knocking, banging, wailing and numerous other noises are reported almost daily. Most visitors have managed to capture globules on their film, and some have even recorded fully manifested ghosts, as well as shadows and imprints of various kinds.

TRAVELOGUE

Day One: Saturday, June 22, 9:30 p.m.

We took the winding road down to the ferry, and boarded the very last boat of the night. A long stream of cars followed us aboard, where we were instructed to turn off our engines and headlights. Once parked, we noticed a small number of odd bugs starting to gather. By the time we were well out onto the river, some locals began standing outside their cars, drinking beers and talking, not bothered at all by the bugs landing on them and getting caught in their hair. Crossing the Mississippi, so late at night, was a bit scary. We all had envisioned a peaceful slow ride across the beautiful river, which we expected to exude a dark and quiet atmosphere. Instead, the Ferry pushed full speed carrying close to fifteen vehicles, reaching the other side in an unbelievably short amount of time. The river was hardly visible and the floodlights illuminated the millions of flying unidentified insects, which were attaching themselves to everything, including our windshield. Suffice to say, by the time we reached the other side, all three of us were shaken up and all romanticism about floating across the lazy Mississippi had come to a screeching halt.

We disembarked, and drove down a dark road lined

with oak trees and dangling Spanish Moss. Finally, we arrived at The Myrtles Plantation, which is now a Bed and Breakfast. The Carriage House Restaurant, on the property but separately owned, was closing up and everyone was leaving. We went to check in, and I was out of the car for no more than three minutes, when something unseen bumped into me. I sensed a ghost jeering at us, and I shivered when I told Shante what I had just felt. The plantation was teeming with paranormal activity, and with all the residual energy that was permeating everything, I was barely able to walk.

Nailed to the door of the Reservations Office was an envelope, with two keys and a note saying that the staff had waited for us until dark, and then gone home. The message told us to go to the caretaker's house in back, and ask for Coco, in the event of an emergency. None of the guestrooms had phones.

We explored the plantation on our way to the "slave quarters," where one of our rooms, "The Azalea Room," was located. This was the first in a chain of rooms attached to the rear of the restaurant. The Azalea Room was small, with an oversized bed, a table, two chairs, and a very small bathroom. It was nothing special, and didn't even have a TV. One of the room's two doors led to the back lawn area, and the other to the parking lot.

We had also reserved "The General Bradford Suite,"

which was like a small apartment. Located on the main floor at the end of the plantation, it was absolutely beautiful. A massive door opened onto a beautiful parlor, with a fireplace, velvet couches and a loveseat. A small, dainty, crystal chandelier hung elegantly from the ceiling. Pale green carpeting, flowing drapes and a decorative table accented the room's elaborate style. Everything had been designed with care and class, but conveyed a masculine, rather than a feminine feeling. The bathroom, off to the left, was nice, but basic. The bedroom was amazing. It faced the front porch, and had a view of the front lawn. The ceilings were fourteen feet high; two windows were hung with dramatic red drapes, trimmed and corded in gold; and there was a massive four-poster bed, a fireplace, another chandelier, and a fainting couch covered in beige velvet, accompanied by an antique oak vanity.

We unpacked, and ventured out into the warm night air. A group of women were seated in the rocking chairs on the back porch. They asked to see our suite, and as we showed it to them, they whispered tales about people being awakened in the middle of the night by the coughing of the long-dead General Bradford. They found a locked door, which led to Mrs. Sterling's private bedroom. According to rumor, she likes to wake people at night, from this adjacent room, by moving chairs around, clattering objects, and tossing things onto the floor.

Behind the house is a fairly large swamp. A small, arched, wooden bridge provides a path to a tiny island, where a secluded white gazebo is nestled among the shrubs. At night, we found the old wooden bridge a bit treacherous. On the way back, it was too dark to see very well, and I tripped over one of the bridge's broken wooden steps, resulting in a couple of scrapes and a nasty bruise on my knee. There are also patches of poison ivy, reaching out to grab any available bare legs. Explorers beware: nighttime is not the best time to familiarize yourselves with the property. That night, Shante slept in the Azalea Room, and Maliena and I slept in The Bradford Suite. We settled in and turned out the lights. The darkness felt like a thick blanket that entombed us. We stared into the pitch, black room with the covers pulled up to our noses. My eyes played tricks on me and we both held our breath every time we heard the slightest noise, finally daylight started to seep in through the thick yards of drapery, and we were able to fall asleep.

Day Two: Sunday, June 23, 8:45 a.m.

Shante woke us for breakfast. She reported that she had not slept very well the night before, because of the strange, tapping noises she had heard all night. She was too scared to investigate, and spent the night tossing and turning, constantly harassed by the steady knocks and taps. For someone who rarely sees or hears anything paranormal, it was frightening! We had breakfast outside, with some of the other guests, and a woman staying a few doors down from the Azalea Room mentioned that she too had heard these noises. In fact, after midnight she had gone outside to try and find out what it was, but had no luck locating the source.

We took the organized tour of the main house, which is a museum now, and learned many interesting facts. The interior of the home was very grand. We toured the formal dining room, the game room, Mrs. Sterling's suite, and the "his and her" parlors for entertaining. The home is filled with hand painted wall paper, Aubusson tapestries, Baccarat crystal chandeliers, Carrera marble mantles and gold leafed French period furnishings. At the end of the tour, the guide told us she would give me the keys to the main house, when she left for the day. Prior to our arrival, we had obtained special permission to enter this area at night. Normally, it is closed to the public, except for the guided tours during the day.

We ate lunch at the Ox Bow Carriage House Restaurant, which has the best food in Louisiana, hands down! After lunch, we ventured into Saint Francisville, to do some exploring. We headed back to the plantation around 4:00 p.m.

The day was winding down, the restaurant was slow, and the guests were few. We went walking through the grounds while there was still daylight, and found an old swimming pool that had gone to waste; it actually looked like it had never been completed. It was filled with dark swamp water, and turtles were sitting poolside. Standing a little way off, was another old, dilapidated, original building. We walked around to the back road. Beautiful trees towered above us. Eventually, we walked around to the back of the swamp, then returned to the main house. We relaxed in the back-porch rocking chairs, basking in the plantation's lazy atmosphere.

Fern, the employee working that day, gave me the keys to the museum area, and also to an unoccupied upstairs bedroom. Originally the children's nursery, it was now called "The William Winters Room." The energy was strong there, and I could really pick up on the essence of the two children. The room was average-sized, with a big, walk-in closet and bathroom. An adjoining door led to the next guestroom, which was bolted. The William Winters Room is the room where guests have reported being disturbed by children playing and jumping on the bed.

We soon headed back downstairs to the rocking chairs, where we could overlook the grounds. Two men arrived, and said they were spending the night with a small group, in hopes of seeing some ghosts. After the employees left for the night, the only ones still remaining on the vast plantation were the caretaker, the three of us, two couples, two girlfriends from Boston, and the small group with the two men. There are no televisions or telephones on the property, so everyone comes to go ghost hunting.

At first, we were all spread out. I went inside to shower, Shante and Maliena went down to the Azalea Room, and everyone else was combing the grounds. Shante and Maliena had gone to the car, which was parked in front of the Azalea Room's door. They were casually talking and rummaging through their things, when all of a sudden they heard the infamous tapping. It lasted about thirty seconds, and then stopped. Overcome with curiosity, the girls tried to locate the source. It seemed to be coming from behind a bush, which was against a wall that separated the restaurant from the rooms. Shante said that when it first started, it seemed very methodic, like faint hammering against the wall. The tapping could have been coming from the restaurant, but it was Sunday night, and the restaurant was closed until Tuesday. As they listened and stared at the wall, the tapping became irregular and wild. After a minute, it stopped. Being a smart-ass, Maliena half-jokingly walked over to the wall and tapped three times. A split second later, her tap was mimicked back, with three swift taps. Shante's eyes widened, as she pointed and said, "See, I heard that all night!" Testing fate again, Maliena walked closer and tapped once more, a hard, solid tap. The exact same sound was returned. Both girls jumped, it startled them so much. Shante began to call out, and they looked behind the building. They said they kept thinking, "No way could that tapping be random; either someone is back there playing a really good joke on us, or it's a ghost." (Later, when I heard the story, I assured them it was not a joke.) For a moment, all was silent, but when they started to walk away, the tapping noise exploded into a barrage of sporadic beats. It lasted long enough for Shante to run and grab our audio recorder, but as soon as she turned it on, the noise stopped. Carefully, she placed the recorder by the bush, and hid it under the grass. Maliena returned to her room to take a bath, and Shante came up to my suite, leaving Maliena alone. Halfway through her bath, Maliena said the tapping started again; she could hear it loudly, but it was the methodic tapping they had heard at first. By the time she finished and dressed, the tapping had stopped.

Maliena went outside, grabbed the recorder and headed back to the main house. It was barely dusk, but one couple was already outside, snapping photos and showing off all sorts of pictures of the light orb's they were catching with their digital camera. The two men in the group from upstairs had captured some sort of disembodied voice on their recorder, actual audible words being whispered while they were spoken. They had been trying to call out to a spirit, and had asked to speak with Judge Woodruff. The voice on the recorder said, "I'm Woodruff." But Judge Woodruff didn't die on the plantation, or haunt it! They had mixed up the facts: it was General Bradford who is said to haunt the plantation. I believe that they actually did pick up a paranormal energy, but the ghost to whom they were speaking was not the Judge.

When a person calls in entities, they risk being lied to. It is not uncommon for a wayward spirit to lie and try to trick the living. This is one reason why I encourage people to leave Ouija boards, and other conjuring instruments, alone, unless they are capable of dealing with the possible consequences. People can unknowingly open themselves up to possessions, and other dangers, by communicating with ghosts and entities. The men also said that during their attempt to contact the spirit, they had not heard anything. It was when they replayed the tape, they realized they had picked up a voice.

We listened to our own tape, and discovered we had recorded two things. The first was some sort of screeching or wailing sound, although I haven't decided the origin of it. The second was the tapping, with an overlay of crickets singing. At first, the tapping sounded the same-rhythmic and slow—but as we listened, we started to hear lower taps, which began to transform into what I can only describe as a drumming, like a voodoo ceremony where participants use their hands to strike the traditional drums. It was very wild, and totally unexpected. I know that it was not a machine or a figment of our imagination. We have the tape as our proof. The first tapping sounds that Maliena and Shante had heard were continuous and slow; but the beating drums on the audiotape had about three different sources, with different volumes and ranges overlaying the tapping. The drumming was not just rhythmic, but musical as well.

Later, the three of us ventured back to the Azalea Room, because I wanted to hear the noise for myself. We waited a long time, and heard nothing; then it started again, right before we left. This time, it was not like it had been before or how it had been on the tape. There were only a few knocks, and then it stopped. I called out, and heard no response. We tried tapping back, and almost immediately heard a response. Once, the response mimicked ours. The next time, it almost seemed to complete the knocks we sent first. Shante walked up to Coco's door and knocked, but no one opened it. She asked, through the door, if anyone had ever reported these sounds, coming from this wall before. "It's a dripping water pipe," someone said. The last time I checked, water pipes didn't answer you back. We stayed in the Azalea Room for awhile, and finally decided to head back to the main house.

When I prayed for answers about the noises, and asked my angels and spirit guides to help clarify where these beats were coming from, I received some startling information. I was told that the tapping was coming from a location that existed back in the 1800's, a time when the slaves would hold their voodoo ceremonies and festivals. Because The Myrtles Plantation contains a vortex, what we were tapping into was a small tear in our dimension that opened a passageway to another time and space. We actually had been able to hear something, not from a ghost, but from living people in another dimension. On their side of the dimension, they were performing a ceremony and receiving our knocks as confirmation of the spirit world acknowledging them. On our side, we received their knocks and drum recordings as confirmation that other dimensions simultaneously exist. Or that time is not as we think it to be. The past, present, and future are all one in the spirit world. Think of time as an onion with layers that go into a circular motion. This was an incredible revelation.

The vortex provides some sort of portal, which carried these sounds from a different time dimension back and forth. It's so amazing to think that our beats were being brought to them as well. Both groups were standing on the same land, but in a different place in time, sacred burial land to boot. Who did they think was responding to them? Certainly not three women from the future! If only we could have seen each other. Heart attacks for everyone, I'm sure.

Later, we were able to verify that at one time this area had indeed been an open field, with cabins where the slaves would hold their ceremonies. That was really all the proof we needed to support the accuracy of my information.

The last guests for the night had arrived, and were busy collaborating with each other about what they hoped to see or record. We were standing in the foyer of the main house, talking to one of the men about our experiences thus far, when I felt the back of my skirt being lifted up. I turned to shoo Maliena away, because I thought she was teasing me. The look on her face told me immediately that it had not been her joke. Maliena eyes were bigger than golf balls, and her mouth had dropped open. She was staring at the back of my skirt. "Oh my God," she stammered. "Michelle, did you feel that?" "Yes," I said. "I thought you were pulling on me." Eyes still wide, she said, "It wasn't me, but I was looking at the door and I saw your skirt being pulled up by an invisible hand." She said that it was just as if someone had walked up and pulled my skirt straight out, only no one was there. She kept on about how she had seen it, "plain as day." I began to feel for the room's energy, and psychically saw the ghost of the little girl behind the piano, giggling before she disappeared. This had obviously been her idea of a practical joke. Four of us were standing there, and no one else had seen anything. But everyone agreed that Maliena had not touched me. We were all a little spooked by this encounter, so we headed upstairs.

The two men we had first met had invited us to their suite, and when we entered we were surprised to see eight people already there, looking at photographs and checking out video and audio recordings. They asked if I would be willing to try a séance, and after much coercion, I reluctantly agreed. I had two main concerns: first, in this sort of environment, with so much paranormal activity, you don't know who or what you might attract; second, I didn't know any of the people there, and I felt a great responsibility for everyone's safety. The last thing I needed was a sudden possession or accident to befall one of the guests. Shante was especially eager for a séance, and since we were all consenting adults, I finally gave in to her pestering.

Eleven of us walked into the hallway foyer, and gathered on the floor. I asked everyone to form a circle and hold hands. I then told them to pray for protection, and to welcome any spirits they wished to contact. Right away, Maliena got an image of Chloe, not because she wanted to contact her, but more like the vision just popped into her head. Then, Maliena's left ear began to ache. At this point, we invited Chloe's ghost to come in and talk with us, but I felt that Chloe was already there. The air chilled a little, and when I looked around, I saw Chloe fading in and out of the corner. I pointed to where the spirit of Chloe was standing, and Maliena quickly got up to snap several photos.

When the film was developed, there were signs that Chloe had indeed been present. In each picture, a pinpoint of white light showed up, and in each picture the light seemed to move in an downward direction. In the last picture, the pinpoint of light had begun to trace the outline of an oval, right where her head would have been. Our eyes wide with anticipation, we spent the next few minutes hoping to see or hear something. But aside from our breathing, the room remained silent.

For a few minutes, I spoke to everyone about ghosts and hauntings. I answered a number of questions, and also picked up on one gentleman's family member who had "come in," but was not wayward. I decided we wouldn't get any further this night, because the people in the circle were of different energies, and not at all like-minded. I could hear their thoughts, and knew that a smaller group of guests, with more positive outlooks, would have ensured a better outcome.

We ended the séance, and broke the circle to head back downstairs. Since the plantation had kindly provided me with the keys to the main museum, I did a walk-through before we all met back on the porch. For the next few hours, people drifted in and out of their rooms and around the grounds. I took some time to speak to one of the girls who had recently lost a good friend, and a few of the guests borrowed our flashlights and made their way to the swamp. Unfortunately, the only thing that was frightening them, were each other!

At one point, when the three of us had returned to the main museum entrance, one of the glass doors began to rattle ominously. Maliena tried to get it on audio, but it didn't pick up. It was now almost three in the morning, we were all exhausted, and I started to think that with so many people around, it would be impossible to see anything paranormal. Knowing our odds were slim, we retired to the General Bradford Suite to rest. Shante lay down on the fainting couch and Maliena crawled on to the main bed. I told the girls that I wanted to walk through one more time, and that I would be back later. I wandered around the grounds, searching for any supernatural signs, accompanied by the two girls from Boston and a few of the men. I took them to the Azalea Room, hoping to hear the tapping. We waited for fifteen minutes, but heard nothing. Returning to the main house, we decided to walk around to the front verandah. As I gazed out into the fragrant myrtle trees, which lined the front of the plantation, I started to see a luminescent, glowing orb, drifting in and out. At first, I didn't mention it to anyone; I just felt mesmerized by it. As I looked more closely, I began to see a pair of eyes peering out at me. A bit startled, I glanced around to see if anyone else had noticed. The two girls pointed to the orb and asked if I could see anything. I said, "yes," and explained what I was seeing. The rest of the group told me they could definitely sense something out there, but they couldn't see it. One of the girls had a night vision video camera, and I told her to record the area. She complained that her camera wouldn't focus, but I told her to film anyway, knowing that she would undoubtedly capture something. She rewound the film and watched. Sure enough, a small glowing orb came into view; it lasted for a few seconds, and then disappeared. Then I began to see the eyes even more clearly, glinting out at us. The ghost that was lurking in the shadows appeared to be as curious as we were, and became bolder, and more visible. I was still the only person who could see anything, but the camera appeared to be doing a good job of recording, so I told the girl to film the same spot again. Her lens went out of focus for a minute or so, and then refocused automatically. When she rewound the film, for the second time, what we saw was unbelievable!

The camera had recorded a blur, which lasted only a moment. It then refocused, exposing a glowing white globule, bouncing between two of the myrtle trees. Halfway to the second tree, the orb began to take shape. Within a split second, we saw this glowing ball of white light, the size of a basketball, shift into an average-sized black man! The ghostly figure was so defined, I could see his skin color, his brown pants, and his cream-colored shirt. He walked maybe three or four steps, dematerialized back into the orb, floated past the tree, and disappeared. Never in my life have I ever seen anything so incredible. It was the most real, most indescribable image I have ever seen on film. I rushed back to our room, and woke Shante and Maliena to tell them about it. They ran out to the porch to get a first-hand look, and were totally awed.

Shante and I stayed outside for another hour, but Maliena went back to bed. She couldn't imagine anything being able to top this experience.

Shante headed back to the Azalea Room, feeling really spooked. She had heard the voodoo drum recording, and seen the ghost video on the front lawn, and was not too thrilled about sleeping alone. Earlier, she had asked me to leave the outside light on, and I had done so; but when she headed back to her room, everything was pitch black. Hurriedly, she jammed her key into the lock, opened the door, and turned on every light. She went to sleep, but left the bathroom light on, all night.

Day Three: Monday, June 24

When we woke up this morning, everyone had a story to tell, but none as good as the one about the video. All over the plantation, tired guests were suffering the effects from the hustle and bustle of the night before. Men and women dragged themselves from their rooms, trying to enjoy the breeze before the temperature soared into the 90's. The kitchen and the gift-shops were filled with whispered tales about the previous evening's adventure.

We returned our keys to the front desk, packed our belongings, and said goodbye to this extraordinary plantation, and all its paranormal glory.

The girl from Boston with the night vision camera promised to send us a copy of the video, after she returned home; but that was months ago, and we still have not received it.

CHANNELED INFORMATION

The plantation is a cluster of paranormal phenomenon. The main ghosts that haunt the premises are Chloe, the two children, the male presence of General Bradford, and the groundskeeper.

Chloe is generally remorseful about what she did, and she still looks after the children and loves them. She was not killed at the plantation, despite various rumors about being hanged from a myrtle tree. The other slaves did, in fact, drag her to the Mississippi River, where she met her demise.

The children still love to play pranks, and frequent the rooftop to watch people come and go. They press against the windows in the main house, leaving tiny, visible handprints.

There is a vortex in the backyard, enabling ghosts to go in and out. More than anything, this vortex seems to be like an amplifier, which pushes and sucks noises from two separate dimensions back into each other. After I prayed, and channeled what I could from my guides, I am positive that the knocking we heard comes from a dimensional tear. Perhaps this is just a time lapse, from the plantation's earlier years until now, but in any case, the noise we made in response was also heard on the other side, in another time. That is why the knocking answered back the way it did. It's kind of amazing to think that somewhere in the past, or a different place in time, there is a group of people who believe they too are contacting long-dead ancestors, or perhaps some sort of deity.

There is also a black man haunting the premises, who is responsible for showing up in front of the plantation and telling people it is closed. That has been documented several times. He is the same ghost that manifested for us the night before we left. At one time, he was a slave at The Myrtles, and his job was that of groundskeeper. He doesn't like all the activity around the plantation, caused by the living, but he tolerates it. At times, he is a bit grumpy, but he is not harmful.

In the yard in back of the plantation, there is also a bleed-through of soldiers from the Spanish-American War.

The paranormal energy level is higher at The Myrtles than anywhere else I have ever been. This plantation truly deserves its reputation as "America's Most Haunted Home".

I hope that my readers enjoyed our journey. When we first began this endeavor, my primary goal was to experience American history in a very unique way. Because I have the ability to communicate with the dead, I knew that traveling to different haunted locations would enable me to receive enlightening information from deceased people who had lived in many different eras. But almost instantly I realized that this trip would have a much bigger purpose: To allow me to write about ghosts and why they are here, thereby educating people about their existence.

Although paranormal activities are a big part of the metaphysical world, in most circles, talking about ghostly behavior is often taboo. I would like those who read my book to walk away with a better understanding of an area that until recently was chalked up to spooky legends people were fearful of. Actually, ghosts are rather common, but a general lack of insight about them has resulted in various misconceptions. Many people think that all ghosts are malicious, spiteful, and innately evil. But I have found the opposite to be true. In most cases, the ghosts that I have encountered have been shy and scared; not the villains we make them out to be. Once, these ghosts were like you and me. They have simply lost their way home. When you look at them from this perspective, it is easier to have compassion.

Within a two-week period, I witnessed some amazing events. On the "Queen Mary", friendly ghosts granted us access into a forbidden area, revealing to us the bowels of the ship. A place not many are able to go alone. In Goldfield Nevada, the middle of nowhere, we experienced one of the most powerful vortexes on earth. In Flagstaff Arizona, I was able to take a breather at the illustrious Monte Vista Hotel. We even left with our first photographed ghost! The history of Tombstone Arizona, proved well worth the detour. To see those buildings and walk into saloons that once housed legendary icon's of the Wild West. We discovered that in those days, women had two choices; either be a housewife, or a legal prostitute. Walking inside of the brothels and looking at these women's photographs still hanging on the wall was mystifying. Cloudcroft New Mexico, was nearly 10,000 feet above sea level, and reminded me of paradise on earth; I felt like I could touch the sky. As for our final destination, "The Myrtles," it turned out to be my favorite place of all. Hands down, this was the location with the most paranormal activity. It was there that we witnessed the incredible sight of glowing orb, manifesting into a man and then changing back into an orb. Our audio recordings also picked up sounds of voodoo drums, coming from another dimension in time and space. (Biggest added bonus at "The Myrtles"...the best food in Louisiana! I intend to return for a vacation, very soon.) The success of this trip has resulted in the planning of "Ghost Stalker Two – Europe," where I look forward to venturing into hidden castles and haunted pubs.

Don't forget your nightlight this evening...and Sleep Well!

In Love and Light,
Michelle Whitedove

For actual photographs and audio recordings of this trip, visit: www.MichelleWhitedove.com

Fear not death,
for the sooner we die
the longer we shall be immortal.
— Benjamin Franklin

HAUNTED HOTEL RESOURCES

Hotel Allegro
171 West Randolph Street
Chicago, IL 60601
800.643.1500
www.allegroChicago.com

The Lodge
1 Corona place
Cloudcroft, NM 88317
800.395.6343
www.thelodge-nm.com

Goldfield Hotel
US Hwy 95
Goldfield, NV 89013

Monte Vista Hotel
100 San Francisco St.
Flagstaff, AZ 86001
928.779.6971
www.hotelmontevista.com

The Pavillion Hotel
833 Poydras St.
New Orleans, LA 70112
504-581-3111
www.LePavillion.com

Birdcage Theater
517 Allen St.
Tombstone, AZ 85638
520.457.3421
www.virtualguidebooks.com
www.tombstone.org

Queen Mary
1126 Queens Hwy.
Long Beach, CA 90802
562.435.3511
www.queenmary.com

The Myrtles
7747 US Hwy 61
PO Box 1100
St. Francisville, LA 70775
225-635-6277
www.myrtlesplantation.com

Naturally gifted since childhood, Michelle Whitedove is a renowned psychic-medium and channel. Currently the host her own TV Talk Show, she also teaches spiritual development courses, conducts personal counseling sessions, and lectures across America. With psychic insight she uses her gifts to relay conversations from the spirit world to those open to hear the profound truth. Conveying not only personal messages but more importantly, greater messages to illuminate the path toward self-growth. Her mission is to empower humanity, to bestow the knowledge that we have unlimited potential and that we do indeed survive the transition that we call death.

Whitedove has been featured on ABC, CBS, FOX, and PBS television and has done many interviews in America as well as Europe.

For more information and a list of public appearances **www.MichelleWhitedove.com**

Prayer for the Dead

Though lost to us, our dead have not forsaken us.

They cannot forget us, as we do not forget them.

They are near us and with us,

and see us through our bodily veil.

Death has silenced them.

They speak not with tongues.

They have cast off the vesture of flesh and

their souls hold their communion with our souls.

They care for us, they feel for us, and they bless us.

They long for us and love us,

as we long for them and love them.

They are ours, as we are theirs.

Death has not dissolved our union.

- Excerpt of a Zoroastrian Prayer